SEMAINE D'AVIATION de LYON

DU 7 AU 15 MAI

1910

200,000 F. DE PRIX

BILLETS D'ALLER ET RETOUR POUR LYON

ÉMISSION A PARTIR DU 4 MAI. VALIDITÉ JUSQU'AU 19 MAI

Contents

Cover: Painting of an air battle
over the Somme in 1918 between
German Albatros and British Martin-
syde aircraft
Front endpaper: French air display
poster
Rear endpaper: American pioneer
Robert H.Goddard with the world's
first liquid-fuel rocket, 1926

Copyright © 1971: Sir Robert Saundby
First published 1971 by Macdonald
St Giles House 49 Poland St London W1
in the British Commonwealth and
American Heritage Press
551 Fifth Avenue New York NY 10017
in the United States of America
Library of Congress Card Catalogue
Number: 70-170177
Made and printed in Great Britain by
Purnell & Sons Ltd Paulton Somerset

EARLY AVIATION
Man Conquers the Air

Air Marshal Sir Robert Saundby

Library of the 20th Century
Macdonald/American Heritage

Chapter 1
In the Beginning

Almost from the beginning of recorded history man has realised the overwhelming advantages conferred by flight and long before it became possible for him to do so in reality traversed the air in his imagination. Among the legends of ancient Greece is the story of the magician and mechanical genius Daedalus who with his son Icarus set off to fly from Crete to the mainland with wings of feathers, fixed to their arms with wax. His father warned Icarus of the danger of flying too high lest the heat of the sun should melt the wax, but in the exhilaration of flight the young man forgot all that he had been told. His wings came unstuck and he fell to his death. There can hardly be anyone familiar with flying during the first quarter of this century who has not known a tragedy caused by much the same blend of zeal and inexperience.

It is remarkable how often these flights of imagination have come close to the facts of flight as we now know them. In the *Arabian Nights Entertainments* there are two references to flying. Sindbad the Sailor tells of the destruction of his ship by aerial bombardment. He describes how the crew saw two rocs, immense birds, 'flying towards us, carrying great stones . . . in their fearful claws. They hovered just over the ship, and then one of them let fall a stone which, however, missed the ship and fell into the sea which dashed up like a great wall of water. But the other roc, unhappily, aimed better, and dropping his enormous stone into the very middle of the ship splintered her into a thousand pieces.' The crew were thrown into the water and the victorious birds flew away and soon disappeared from sight. This must be the earliest reference to air bombardment, and almost every air/sea battle since has followed a similar pattern.

The second reference in the *Arabian Nights* is to the magic carpet of Bisnagar, which carried its passengers, seated upon it, and floated through the air at a low height, much as the hovercraft does today.

Left: H.J.Turner's 'Lament for Icarus' — first victim of man's lust to fly, Icarus demonstrated a common error of air pioneers: his enthusiasm dangerously exceeded his technical know-how

In 1727 Jonathan Swift, in *Gulliver's Travels,* described the flying island of Laputa, the residence of the ruler of Balnibarbi and his government, which was much like a huge space-station in earth orbit. Swift realised the great advantages of such a flying island. He writes: 'If any town (in the King's dominions below) should engage in rebellion or mutiny, fall into violent factions, or refuse to pay the usual tribute, the King has two methods of reducing them to obedience. The first and mildest course is by keeping the island hovering over such a town and the lands about it, whereby he can deprive them of the benefit of the sun and the rain, and consequently afflict the inhabitants with dearth and diseases: and if the crime deserve it, they are at the same time pelted from above with great stones, against which they have no defence but by creeping into cellars and caves, while the roofs of their houses are beaten to pieces. But if they still continue obstinate, or offer to raise insurrections, he proceeds to the last remedy by letting the island drop directly upon their heads, which makes an universal destruction both of houses and men.' And in 1750 Robert Paltock wrote a book called *The Life and Adventures of Peter Wilkins,* a remarkable story about a race of imaginary flying 'Indians' — human beings equipped with bat-like wings. In this book the author shows a considerable understanding of the possibilities of gliding flight.

As early as 1648 the Englishman John Wilkins, a founder member of the Royal Society, had written a percipient paper on human flight. He realised the difficulties of supporting the weight of a man and his flying mechanism in so thin and light a body as the air, but he had watched soaring birds and seen how easily they rode the air with little if any perceptible motion of the wings. With a machine of the right proportions, operated by someone with the necessary skill and experience, he believed that it would be possible to emulate the birds. The main difficulty, he thought, would be raising such a machine into the air; once there 'it will be easy, as it is in the flight of all kinds of birds which being at any great distance from the earth are able to continue their motion for a long time and way with little labour and weariness.' But he warned that just as the sails of ships had been perfected by degrees, so must a successful flying machine be evolved by trials and experiments over a long period.

Of course, much thought had already been given to this subject. The eminent philosopher Roger Bacon (1214-94) had designed a 'flying chariot', and that many-sided genius Leonardo da Vinci (1452-1519) had devised a

Right: First flight — September 1783, a balloon built by the Montgolfier brothers rises in the sky above Versailles palace

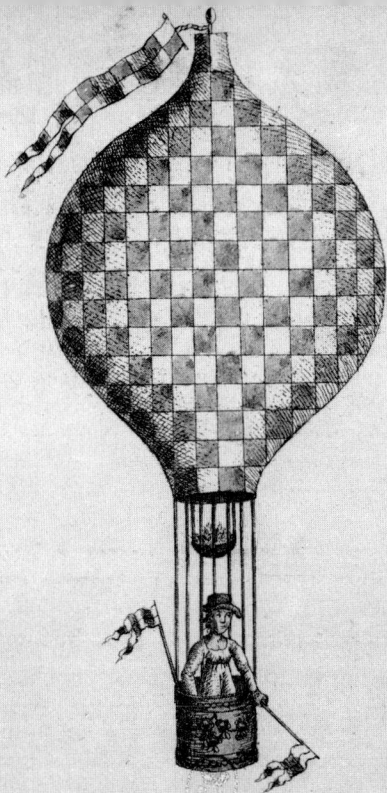

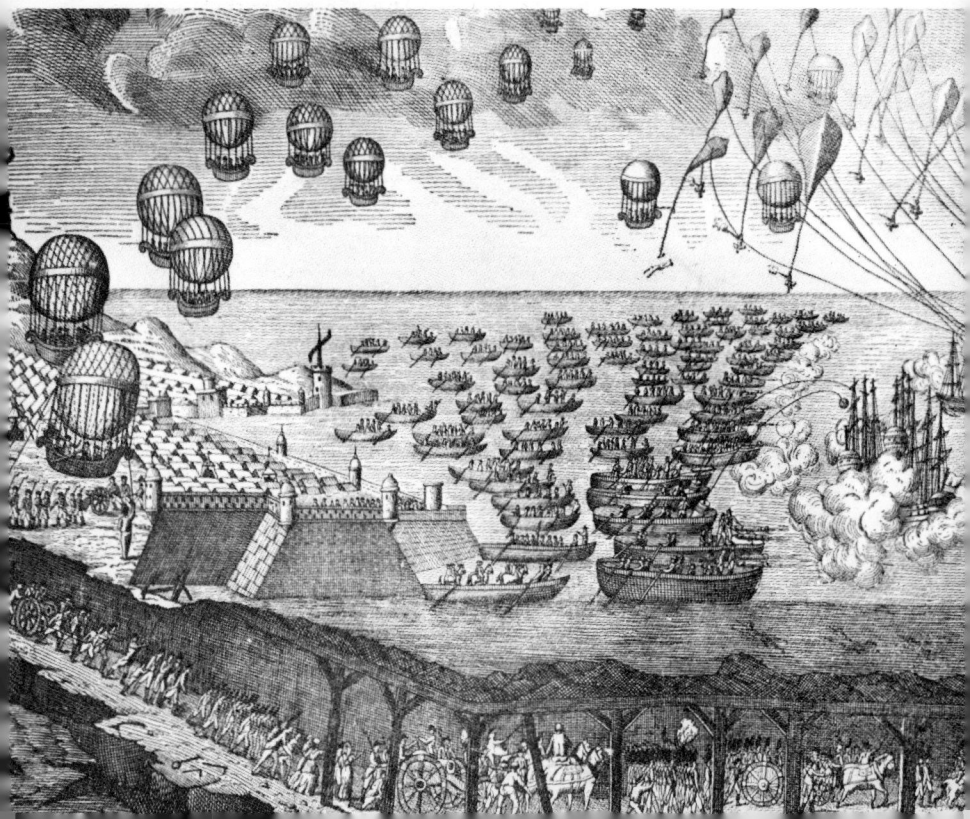

mechanism to enable a man to operate a pair of wings by leg-power. John Damian, a philosopher and physician at the court of James IV of Scotland, made himself a pair of wings, but when in 1507 he launched himself from the wall of Stirling Castle in an attempt to fly, he fell to the ground and was lucky to escape with a broken leg. Much later another such essay was made in Paris in 1742 by the Marquis de Bacqueville, who attempted to fly across the Seine but fell on to a barge and was seriously injured.

John Wilkins's paper of 1648 made a considerable impression on the learned members of the Royal Society, and in 1665 Joseph Granvill allowed full rein to his imagination. He foresaw that the world might be filled with wonders and that 'posterity will find many things that are now but rumours, verified into practical realities. It may be, some ages hence, a voyage to the southern unknown tracts, yea, possibly to the Moon, will not be more strange than one to America . . . and to confer at the distance of the Indies by sympathetic conveyances may be as usual to future times as to us in a literary correspondence.' Now, just over 300 years later, these prophecies have been fulfilled in space travel and radio.

Very little real progress was made for a long time. A professor at the University of Florence, Giovanni Alfonso Borrelli, wrote a treatise in about the middle of the 17th century in which he showed that a bird was in proportion far stronger and lighter than a human being, and that man could never achieve artificial flight by means of his own strength. The truth of this contention was widely accepted, and various proposals for machines, supported by vacuum globes or gas-filled envelopes and propelled by manually-operated paddles or fans, were put forward. Practical difficulties, with the limited mechanical knowledge of the time, prevented the construction of such machines, which never – to use a modern phrase – got further than the drawing board.

The development of aviation was also retarded by moral considerations and feared by both churchmen and philosophers. A Jesuit monk, Francesco Lana, who had himself designed a flying-machine, wrote during the latter part of the 17th century: 'I do not foresee any other difficulties that could prevail against this invention, save one only, which to me seems the greatest of them all, and that is that God would never surely allow such a machine to be successful, since it would create many disturbances in the civil and political governments of mankind. Where is the man who can fail to see that no city would be proof

Top left: Elegance aloft! ***Top right and bottom:*** *During the Revolutionary and Napoleonic wars there were rumours of intended French aerial (and Channel tunnel) invasions*

9

in Wien
1807

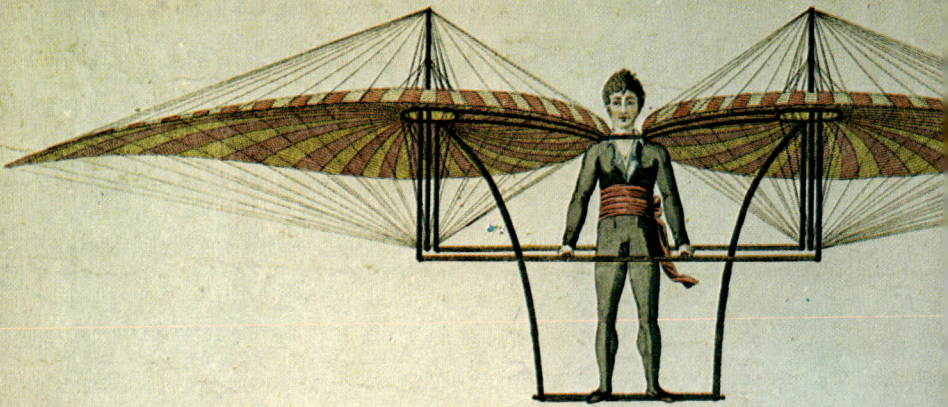

Ansicht der Fläche.

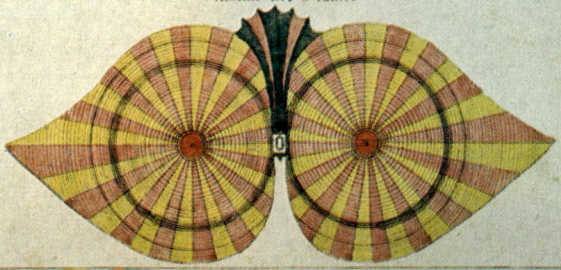

Maasstab zum Profil

4 Schuhe.

against surprise, when the ship could at any time be steered over its squares, or even over the courtyards of dwelling-houses, and brought to earth for the landing of its crew? Iron weights could be hurled to wreck ships at sea, or they could be set on fire by fire-balls and bombs; nor ships alone, but houses, fortresses, and cities could be thus destroyed, with the certainty that the airships could come to no harm as the missiles would be hurled from a vast height.'

This fearsome prediction raised doubts in the minds of many as to the wisdom of attempting to solve the problems of human flight. And the great Samuel Johnson (1709-84), in his novel *Rasselas,* asked where the security of the good would be if the wicked could attack them from the air at will.

The first flight

It was not until the latter half of the 18th century that enough knowledge had been gained to make it possible for men to leave the ground and travel through the air. The earliest means of doing so was the balloon, at first lifted by an envelope filled with hot air. In June 1783 the Montgolfier brothers released a hot-air balloon from the market place at Annonay in France, which quickly ascended to a height of 6,500 feet. Soon afterwards further ascents were made carrying sheep and other animals, all of which returned to earth unharmed. The Montgolfier brothers could have gone up in one of their balloons and thus been the first men to fly, but they did not do so; that honour belongs to two daring Frenchmen, the Marquis d'Arlandes and Pilâtre de Rozier, who made an ascent in a hot-air balloon from Paris in November 1783, returning to earth after a successful and uneventful flight. The era of the lighter-than-air craft had begun.

In August 1784 James Tytler made a flight of half-a-mile in a hot-air balloon in Scotland. The following year Jean-Pierre Blanchard, accompanied by an American, Dr John Jefferies, attracted much public attention by crossing the Channel from Dover to the French coast in a balloon. Later they made the first balloon ascent in the United States in 1793. At the battle of Fleurus, in June 1794, the French republican army used a captive balloon for observation work. However, the sightings of the aeronaut, Captain Coutelle, were not apparently of much consequence.

Blanchard's crossing of the Channel stimulated an imaginative Frenchman named Thilorier, at the turn **15** ▷

Maasstab zur Fläche

Top left: *Inventor Edward Golightly depicted astride his 'rocket'.* **Bottom:** *1807 design for Jacob Degan's flying machine.* **Next page:** *1829 — a wry glance at the future of transport*

11

Scheme
Now who's for Bengal
GRAND
Direct to
Greenwich Hill
LONDON
BATH
IN SIX
for a new Church
Vont you take a hire for
Select Vestry

of the century, to prepare for Napoleon an ambitious plan for a combined air/sea invasion of England. Troops were to be carried in a vast number of balloons and landed on the English coast, presumably to seize a bridgehead for the main sea-borne invasion. Thilorier had an absurdly exaggerated idea of the lifting power of balloons, which in his plan were so heavily loaded with troops and their lavish impedimenta that they could never have left the ground. Napoleon was unimpressed and preferred to rely on more conventional means of transport. He had, however, taken a balloon with him on his expedition to Egypt in 1798-9, but there is no evidence that it was used in operations.

Soon hot air as a lifting agent was replaced by hydrogen gas, the use of which was first suggested in 1767 by Dr Joseph Black of the University of Edinburgh. In 1804 a manned balloon reached a height of 23,000 feet, a record which was not broken until 1862 when a balloon over England went up to 34,400 feet, causing severe discomfort to the aeronauts and putting them in great peril from frostbite and lack of oxygen.

Though man could now leave the ground, these free balloons were only able to drift with the wind. Some sort of propulsion was clearly needed and several engines were designed for the purpose. But all were too heavy and lacked sufficient power. In 1852 Henri Giffard, a French engineer, built a successful man-carrying airship driven by a 3 hp steam engine, but its maximum speed was no more than 6 mph. In 1884 an airship called *La France* was built for the French army; it was 125 feet in length, and was driven by an electric motor of $8\frac{1}{2}$ hp. In 1896 a German, Dr Wölfert, built an airship powered by a Daimler petrol engine, which reached a speed of 9 mph. A second airship was built but caught fire during its trial flight in June 1897 and was destroyed. Dr Wölfert and his assistant lost their lives.

More attention was now given to the development of heavier-than-air flying machines. As early as 1863 several fixed-wing and helicopter-type aircraft had been designed and a few had actually been built, but there was in existence no form of power-plant light enough to lift them into the air. The most promising line of approach, therefore, was to concentrate on gliding flight. The leading exponent of this was a brave and ingenious German named Otto Lilienthal. By 1894 he had gained much knowledge and experience, and was able to rise to a height above that of the point of departure. He regularly made flights of 1,500 feet in length, but was unfortunately

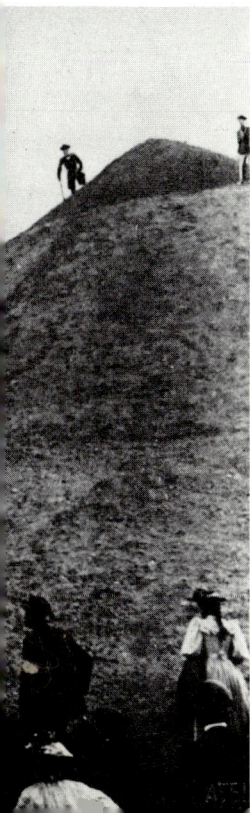

Top left: 1884—the early airship La France. **Bottom:** *German gliding pioneer Otto Lilienthal soars through the air, 1886*

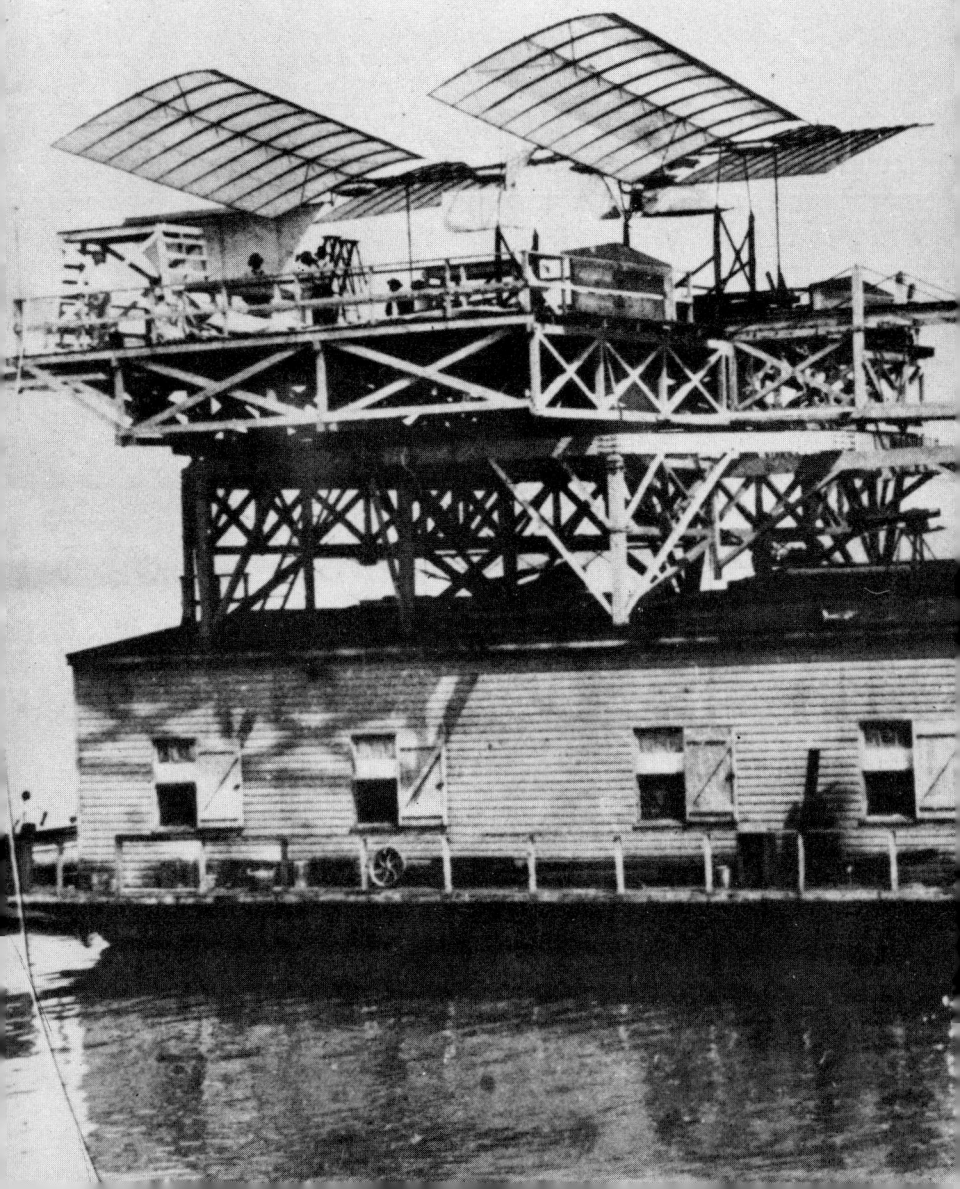

killed in 1896 when one of his gliders broke up in the air.

Inspired by Lilienthal, a lecturer in marine engineering at Glasgow University, Percy Pilcher, began in 1895 to experiment with gliders. He met with considerable success, but anxiety for his safety seems to have held back some of those who might have helped him. Unfortunately, the forebodings of potential patrons like Lord Kelvin were only too well founded, and in September 1899, during a demonstration of his latest glider, the *Hawk,* one of its bracing wires broke and the machine crashed. Pilcher never regained consciousness and died two days later. This seems to be one of the rare examples of progress being retarded by fears of the risks involved.

In the United States Samuel P. Langley had been experimenting since the year 1880 with flying-machines. These were mostly unmanned models powered by elastic motors or compressed air. In 1901 he built a full-sized aeroplane, powered by a very well designed petrol engine developing 52 hp with a weight of only 250 lbs. This machine actually took off, but its control system was defective and it fell into the Potomac River near Washington and was lost.

Hiram Maxim, an American engineer of great resource and ingenuity, also built an aeroplane, and spent much time and effort in the development of light-weight steam engines. He did not, however, attempt to fly this machine, but ran it along between upper and lower rails to test its lifting capacity. These trials proved that it could have lifted itself into the air.

At the turn of the century the prospect of light-weight power plants broadened interest in both lighter-than-air and heavier-than-air machines. The airship (lighter-than-air) seemed to have substantial advantages: it did not have to rely on speed to keep in the air, and it was also more stable and easier to control. Alberto Santos-Dumont, a famous Brazilian engineer, built a number of small airships in France. They were powered by petrol motors, and while some of them met with disaster others were very successful. In 1901 he won the Deutsch prize of 125,000 francs (then worth about £10,000) by flying from Saint-Cloud, circling the Eiffel Tower, and returning to his starting point. The citizens of Paris got to know his little airships well as they often flew at low altitudes round and about the city. And indeed it seemed to many people that the airship was destined to be the air transport vehicle of the future.

Left: American pioneer Langley's Aerodrome aircraft on a houseboat in the Potomac River near Washington DC

Chapter 2

The Conquest of the Air

In 1900 Wilbur and Orville Wright began seriously to study the problems of heavier-than-air craft. They based their work largely on the experiments of Lilienthal and the American inventor Octave Chanute. They built a number of gliders and concentrated on the problems of stability and control. They then built an aeroplane – a biplane equipped with elevator, rudder, and warping wings, powered by a petrol engine driving a pair of airscrews. In December 1903 they made their first flight in this aeroplane at Kitty Hawk, North Carolina. It was immediately successful, largely due to the fact that the Wright brothers realised that the problem was not so much to get an aeroplane into the air as to control it once it was airborne. With an elevator to control movement in the pitching plane, the warping wings to control rolling, and the rudder to provide directional control, they had solved the problem of sustained flight in a heavier-than-air craft.

It was strange that this epoch-making event did not immediately receive the admiration and acclaim that was its due. Of course, almost everybody heard about it, but few people realised the immense importance of the Wright brothers' work. It was generally regarded as a stunt – rather like Blondin's feat in crossing over the Niagara Falls on a tight-rope – a wonderful achievement, no doubt, but one having little application to ordinary human affairs.

Although piloting aeroplanes soon became the passion of a few enthusiasts in many countries, it was mainly – though not always – a rich man's hobby, and flying was confined to races, displays, and demonstrations. A flight by an aeroplane could provide a thrilling climax to a fête or other public gathering, but aviation was not thought of as having any particular commercial or military use.

Nevertheless, the shape of the future was already in being, particularly in the military sphere. Early mili-

Left: 17th December 1903 – watched by his brother Wilbur, Orville Wright makes the historic first flight in a powered heavier-than-air craft on the sand-dunes of Kitty Hawk, NC

tary applications of aviation were mainly ancillary and inoffensive. Balloons filled with hydrogen were first used effectively for reconnaissance during the American Civil War (1861-5). Three freelance aeronauts, the very capable T.S.C. Lowe, with James Allen and John La Mountain, were employed by the Union army. This team made many reconnaissance flights with considerable success. That their work was impeded and finally stopped and has since been largely ignored or glossed over in Civil War histories may be explained by the conservative antagonism of many military authorities to such new-fangled ideas.

During the Franco-Prussian war of 1870 balloons were used during the siege of Paris to convey messages, and sometimes people, in and out of the city. Special light-weight editions of *The Times* newspaper were produced for conveyance by balloon and were available fairly regularly in Paris. The British used balloons and man-lifting kites during the South African War of 1899-1900 for reconnaissance, in order to see, as General Sir Edward Swinton put it, 'the other side of the hill'. Their organisation, under the command of Colonel B.J. Templer of the Balloon Factory at Farnborough, was mobile. The balloons and kites were packed into wagons hauled by steam traction engines. The spherical captive balloons had two drawbacks: they could not be used in a wind of more than 20 mph, and they had an unfortunate tendency to rotate, which made observation difficult. But when the wind became too strong for the balloons to operate, the kites were able to take over. Two or three large box-kites harnessed together were capable of lifting a man with his telephone to a considerable height, but their behaviour was somewhat unpredictable and the observers had an adventurous time. On a rather different level, carrier pigeons had been used successfully to carry messages swiftly over difficult or enemy territory.

The first bombs fall

In the serious application of aviation to military pur-poses, Italy was first in the field. The Italian army had set up an Aeronautical Section at the surprisingly early date of 1884, and had used balloons successfully for reconnaissance during the Eritrean War of 1887-8. But it was during the large-scale Italian army manoeuvres in 1911 that a notable attempt was made to explore the possibilities of military aviation. Two small non-rigid airships and five aeroplanes were used for reconnaissance purposes with very encouraging results. Soon after these

Right: Balloons go to war—a reconnaissance balloon unit accompanies Lord Roberts' advance on Johannesburg, 1900

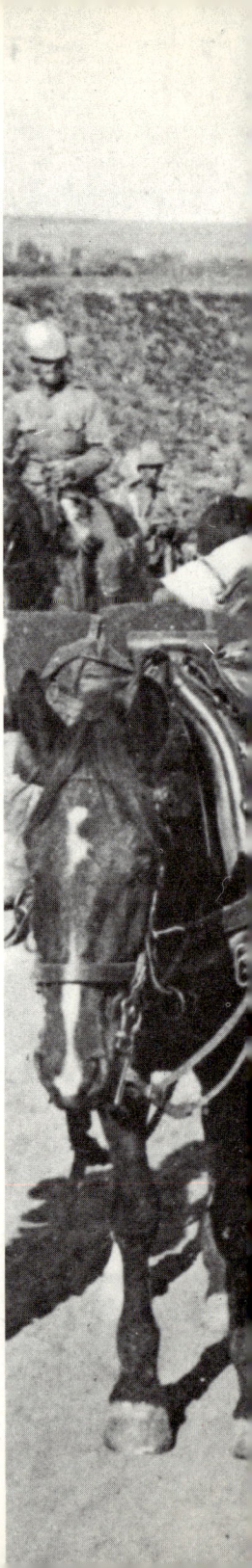

manoeuvres a quarrel arose between Italy and Turkey. In October 1911 war was declared. Italian forces occupied Tripoli; shortly afterwards the Turkish army counter-attacked. The Italians resolved to try out their aircraft in the conditions of actual warfare. Captain Piazza, who enjoyed the magniloquent title of Commander of the Air Fleet, took off for the first wartime flight of an aeroplane on 23rd October 1911. He flew over the Turkish lines, where his appearance caused awe and consternation. On 25th October, Captain Moizo carried out a reconnaissance flight. When over the Turkish positions, his wings were pierced by rifle bullets fired from the ground. They passed harmlessly through the fabric and no serious damage was done.

A further remarkable event occurred on 1st November, when Lieutenant Cavotti dropped four bombs on enemy targets. These bombs were converted Swedish hand-grenades of two kilogrammes weight (4½ lbs), and were simply dropped over the side by hand. During the next few days several more of these bombs were dropped, and before long Turkey protested at the air bombardment of a military hospital at Ain Zara. An impartial inquiry was unable to establish the existence of any sort of hospital at Ain Zara, but it is probable that some of the military tents were occupied by sick and wounded. The Italians were surprised at the Turkish protest and pointed out that the encampment at Ain Zara had been recently bombarded by the Italian navy, firing no less than 152 heavy shells. No protest had been received from the Turks after this bombardment.

There followed a lively discussion in the Italian, Turkish, and neutral Press about the ethics of air bombardment. It is interesting to note that the very first occasion on which bombs were dropped from the air gave rise to an illogical protest, inferring that a few very small aerial bombs were more lethal and devastating than a large number of heavy shells fired from warships. This was the first of a long series of emotional controversies about the propriety of air bombardment.

The six Italian aeroplanes engaged in this campaign seem to have been capably handled by their crews, who surmounted many difficulties with skill and courage. The army authorities acknowledged that they had performed valuable services, and there is no doubt that their success encouraged many in other countries who had faith in the future of military aviation. But naval and military authorities almost everywhere remained apathetic. 26 ▷

Top right: A Clément-Bayard airship looms over turn-of-the-century Paris. Bottom: A treat for the ladies—the Spencer airship on display at Ranelagh Gardens in London, 1903

PARIS AU DEBUT DU XXe SIECLE

Pre-War Aircraft

The Wright brothers' triumph consisted mainly in their ability
to control their craft once it was airborne. And they studied
this technique first on unpowered aircraft such as their first
glider **(1)**, built in 1900, before putting it into practice on their
famous motor-driven biplane **(2)** in 1903. In spite of the Wrights'
success with heavier-than-air craft, development still proceeded
on airships: **(3)** German Zeppelin LZ4 in 1908. In response to
the German lighter-than-air challenge, Britain too developed
military airships such as HM Airship No. 9 rigid type **(4)**. The
Germans also developed a number of fine pre-war aeroplanes,
among them the Albatros-Doppeldecker of 1911 **(5)**. British
ingenuity created both the BE8 **(6)** and 'Baby', an Army war
balloon seen here on display at Aldershot in 1909 **(7)**. The French
had the brilliant Maurice Farman's S7 Longhorn **(8)**, and the
Americans Glen Curtiss' interesting 'pusher' biplane **(below)**,
driven by an engine which was placed behind the pilot's seat.

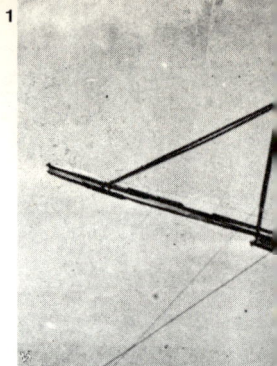

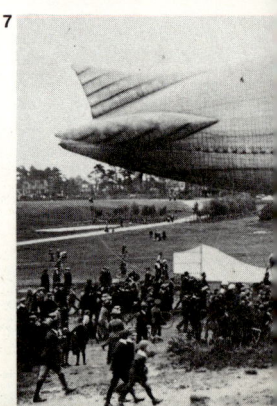

2

4

6

8

In the United States an army air arm had been formed as early as 1907, but it was on a very small scale and progress was so slow as to be almost imperceptible. An Aeronautical Division of the Signal Corps was established in August of that year, responsible for 'balloons, air machines, and all kindred subjects'. At its formation the division possessed only balloons, but in 1908 it acquired a small non-rigid airship. It did not obtain its first aeroplane, a Wright biplane, until August 1909, and this was not joined by another until, early in 1911, one was lent by Mr Robert Collier. In that year a bomb-sight was invented by a former army officer, Riley E. Scott. He offered it to the War Department, who were not interested and declined to purchase it. Scott then took the sight to Europe where it won a substantial money prize in a competition. However, the interest of the military authorities was still not aroused, and none of the embryo air forces of the Continent were willing to buy it.

A Signal Corps Aviation School was set up on North Island, San Diego in December 1913, but at the outbreak of the First World War the US Army air arm had no more than twenty aeroplanes on its strength. By 1914 there was also a small naval air arm, but it is remarkable that America, where the first successful flight of an aeroplane was made in 1903, should have made so little progress in military aviation in eleven years.

The organisation of the army air arm was also far from satisfactory. The US Army pilots soon showed some restiveness at being commanded and administered by the Signal Corps, most of whose senior officers were rigid and unsympathetic. A number of incidents occurred, and an irate signals officer described the airmen as being 'deficient in discipline and the proper knowledge of the customs of the service'. Indeed, it was true that in the newly-fledged air forces of almost all countries the pilots and observers, who tended to be individualistic and even eccentric, were looked upon with a good deal of apprehension by senior army and naval officers.

In France there were a number of enthusiastic civilian pilots and a few keen junior officers of both services who had obtained their pilots' licences, but the naval and army chiefs, when not downright hostile, were apathetic towards military aviation. Naval and army flying services had indeed been formed, but little or no thought had been given to the way in which they should be employed in war. Few, if any, senior officers had any grasp of the functions of military aircraft, and General Foch, a former

Right: Olympia Flight Exhibition of 1910. Only a few short years after the Wright brothers' first flight, the commercial and military development of aircraft was gathering momentum

commandant of the Ecole Supérieure de Guerre, said, 'Aviation is good sport, but for the army it is useless'.

The French High Command, in spite of its great reputation, in fact contained some of the most hidebound and conservative military leaders of the great powers, who were excelled in these respects only by some of those of the United States. The French aviation designers and engineers were, however, quite outstanding. Louis Blériot, Maurice and Henri Farman, the Voisin brothers for aeroplanes, and Renault and the brothers Louis and Laurent Seguin for engines, were famous over the whole world. The quality and performance of the French aircraft and such lightweight air-cooled engines as the Renault and the rotary Gnome and its successors were probably better than those of any other country, and they were extensively used by Britain and later by the United States.

French and German airships

After some early disasters the French also produced several notable airships: *La Patrie* in 1906 and *La République* in 1908. Both ships were of semi-rigid design, and both were wrecked early in their careers. They showed, however, considerable promise, and the Zodiac and Clément-Bayard companies began in 1910 to construct airships for the French armed forces and for foreign buyers. There is no doubt that the successful and very controllable little airships designed and built at the turn of the century by Santos-Dumont had made a considerable impression on the French.

But it was in Germany that the greatest progress was made in the design and construction of airships. After the death of Dr Wölfert, when his airship caught fire in June 1897, the Germans turned away from non-rigid and semi-rigid types for the time being. The first rigid airship, designed and built by David Schwarz, was already nearing completion, and made its first ascent in November 1897. It encountered mechanical trouble and descended rather hurriedly, suffering some damage. A large crowd of people who had gathered to witness the flight were so enraged by this failure that they attacked and destroyed the ship. This was not the only example of crowds in various countries wreaking their vengeance on aircraft, and even aviators, whose performance had disappointed them.

In 1900 Count von Zeppelin began designing large rigid airships, but not until 1908, after some years of difficulty and even disaster, did the German government give him

Right: July 1909 — Louis Blériot skims over the English Channel.
Far right: A salute for the aviator — Blériot and his wife

a grant, which was supplemented by £300,000 raised by public subscription. Zeppelin was a distinguished soldier, who had reached the rank of Lieutenant-General in the German army. He was sixty years old when he began to build airships, but they had engaged his attention for a long time previously. His first ship was very large by any previous standards: 420 feet long and about 38 feet in diameter. It had a rigid aluminium frame divided by bulkheads into seventeen compartments, all of which, except the first and the last, contained a gas-filled balloon or *ballonet*. The whole framework was covered with rubberised cotton fabric. Beneath the main structure was a latticed, fabric-covered aluminium keel, which not only added to its strength but formed a convenient passageway. In the keel were two engine-rooms, each containing a 16 hp Daimler petrol engine driving a pair of small airscrews, one on each side of the keel. Control was effected by elevators and a rudder; there was no need to control an airship in the rolling plane.

The main drawback of a large rigid airship was the difficulty — and sometimes danger — of landing in bad weather conditions. A non-rigid ship could deflate itself at once by means of a ripping panel which allowed the gas to escape and the envelope to collapse. But a rigid ship had to be brought down slowly and very carefully, and was controlled by throwing out ropes which had to be grasped and held by a large ground crew. Even so, damage in these circumstances was regrettably frequent.

The trial flight of the first Zeppelin was successful, apart from a little trouble with the steering gear. It was obvious, however, that the ship was seriously underpowered, and it was soon scrapped. Its successor, of very similar design, had a total of 85 hp, which was a very great improvement. But after many experimental flights, during which much was learned, the ship was wrecked in a storm in 1906.

No less than twenty-five Zeppelins and a few Schütte-Lanz (rigid airships with a wooden framework) were built between 1900 and the outbreak of the First World War in 1914. Their lifting power for those days was very great, and they had a very long range. Some of the luckier ones were extremely successful: No. 11, the *Viktoria Luise,* built in 1912, made over 400 flights, carrying no less than 8,551 passengers, and travelling 29,430 miles. Some of the ships had disastrous endings, but it is worthy of record that no passenger in Zeppelin's airships ever lost his life.

It is interesting to note that the design of subsequent

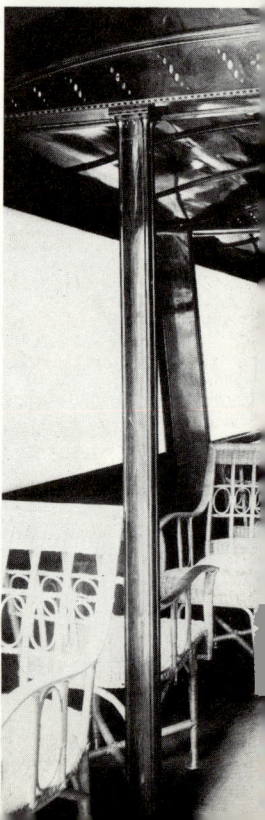

Top right: Count von Zeppelin (in white cap). **Bottom:** *Passenger cabin of the LZ7.* **Far right:** *Zeppelin types from 1900 to 1923*

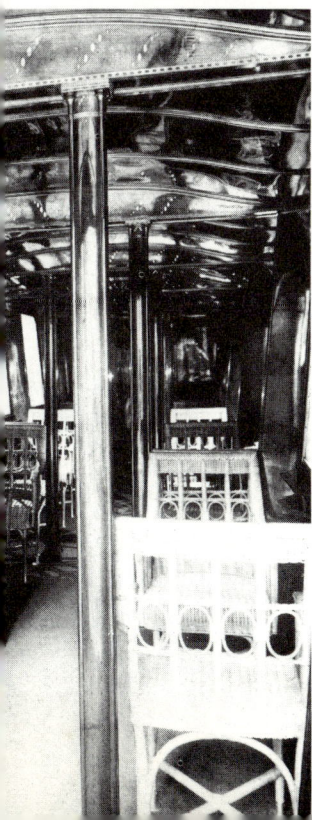

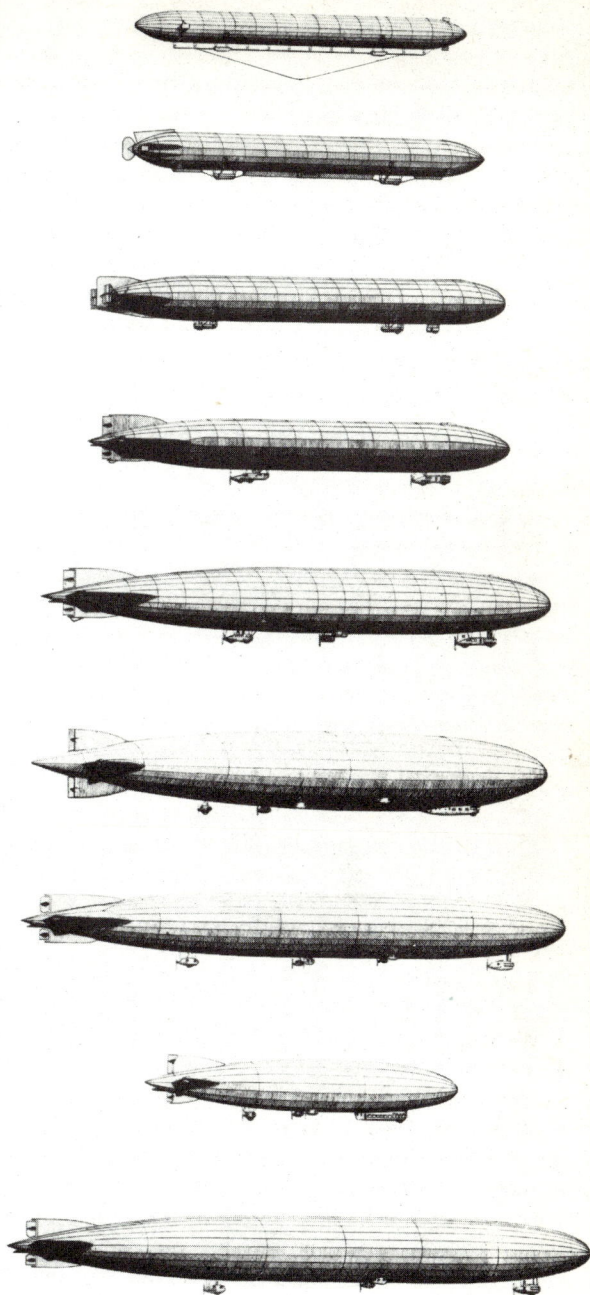

Die wichtigsten Typ-Schiffe
des Luftschiffbau Zeppelin

Zeppelin airships differed but little from the prototype. Zeppelin had thought out his problems very thoroughly before building his first ship. His general principles were so sound that most of them were incorporated in the last airships to be constructed, some thirty years later.

Although the rigid airship attracted most attention in Germany, there was a parallel development of other types of airship—the non-rigid Parseval and the semi-rigid Gross. Major August von Parseval was an infantryman who had retired from the army in 1907 in order to devote himself to aeronautical work. He had already designed a kite-balloon, a type of captive balloon able to fly in strong winds, which was much used for reconnaissance during the First World War, and copied by many other countries. His airships were, perhaps, the best non-rigid ships ever built, and were superseded only because large airships required a rigid structure. In addition, four Gross semi-rigid airships were built. Their performance was outstanding, but even they could not compete with the very large rigid ships built by Zeppelin.

The German navy showed great interest in Zeppelins, which they believed would be useful for sea reconnaissance and even for long-range air bombardment. They therefore relied mainly on lighter-than-air craft, though they possessed a few aeroplanes. The German army also set up an aviation corps, mainly equipped with aeroplanes, as they considered that large airships would be too vulnerable to be of much use in battle zones. They seemed to be a little uncertain about the military functions of aviation, for the army air service was placed under the Inspector-General of Military Transport, which suggests that it was regarded as a means of conveyance. The Germans produced some good early aeroplanes which in the main were heavier and rather faster than their French and British counterparts, and were driven by powerful but relatively heavy water-cooled engines.

The Italians, notwithstanding their early start, had not made very rapid progress by 1914. It is true that the Regia Aeronautica had been set up with a number of enthusiastic and even brilliant pilots, but the senior naval and army officers were, for the most part, rather lukewarm and apathetic. The Italians had no outstanding aircraft designs, but had produced a good engine—the Canton Onné.

In the United Kingdom, although a number of civilians and junior service officers were keen on flying, the Admiralty and War Office were very slow to appreciate the possibilities of military aviation. Not until 1911 was the first unit formed—the Air Battalion of the Royal

Right: A vast hangar for Zeppelin airships in Cologne, 1909

Engineers. It possessed one company of small non-rigid airships, one of aeroplanes, one of balloons, and one of man-lifting kites. The formation of the Air Battalion was a great step forward; until then flying had been the hobby of a few enthusiasts, but now those officers who had trained themselves to fly at their own expense could be absorbed into the army organisation. It was, however, clear to many people that aviation would also be of service to the navy, and in April 1912 the Royal Flying Corps was instituted. It was intended to be a joint service with naval and military wings and a Central Flying School at Upavon on Salisbury Plain manned by officers and men drawn from both services. This plan provided an opportunity for the handful of naval officers who had obtained civilian pilots' licences.

The Central Flying School was a unique organisation. It was commanded by a naval officer, Captain Godfrey Paine, with Major Hugh Trenchard as second-in-command and chief instructor. The instructional staff consisted of army and navy officers, with mechanics seconded from both services. This was an important venture because the Admiralty and War Office had practically no experience of cooperating with each other. But this habit of non-cooperation, which was to prove so calamitous during the Dardanelles campaign, was soon to have no less a disastrous effect on military aviation when, in July 1914, the Admiralty decided to break away and form its own Royal Naval Air Service. The Royal Flying Corps then reverted to the status of a corps of the Army.

In the early history of the development of aviation Britain played a relatively minor part. A few small non-rigid airships had been built, and one large rigid airship, ominously named the *Mayfly*. In fact, she never flew, and was destroyed in a handling accident on the ground in September 1911. At the outbreak of the First World War, the Royal Flying Corps (RFC) and the Royal Naval Air Service (RNAS) had very few aeroplanes that were British-designed and built, and no British aero-engines. They relied heavily on French aircraft and engines and, apart from the excellent Avro, mainly employed products of the Royal Aircraft Factory at Farnborough.

The Avro, ancestor of a long line of successful aircraft —especially the Avro 504—was designed by Mr A.V. Roe, a most able aeronautical engineer. He had flown the first aeroplane over British soil at Brooklands in 1908, in a machine which he had himself designed and built. Even so, it had to rely on a French engine, the 24 hp Antoinette. A later triplane design was powered by a 9 hp JAP motorcycle engine, and was probably the lowest powered aero-

Right: The new 'sport' rapidly became a popular public spectacle

plane ever to leave the ground. In 1910 Roe built the first aeroplane ever to bear the esteemed name of Avro, a very advanced biplane with a 50 hp Gnome engine. This was the well-known 504; soon it was fitted with an 80 hp Gnome. With modifications and improvements this remarkable basic design became famous. Fitted with the 100 hp Mono-soupape engine it was the standard training aircraft of the RFC and RAF for many years. Later versions, with Clerget and radial Bristol engines, lasted well into the 'thirties. It was in use for twenty-five years or more, and became celebrated all over the world.

Shortly before the outbreak of war the British imposed a ban on the further construction and use of monoplanes. There had been several accidents during recent army manoeuvres, some of which had caused the death of well-known aviation enthusiasts. The fact that a high proportion of these accidents occurred to monoplanes gave rise to an idea that this type of aeroplane was unusually dangerous. An outcry in the Press and questions in Parliament led to the imposition of the ban. The total number of accidents was too small to be statistically significant, and there is little doubt that the ban was the result of a hasty and uninformed appreciation of the situation. Britain was the only country to introduce such a measure.

Since the first successful airships at the beginning of the century, and the first aeroplane flight of the Wright brothers in 1903, the development of aviation had been along two main lines. The civil side, since there was as yet no demand for air transport, was confined to displays, air races, giving 'joy-rides', and so forth; enthusiasts, rich and poor, bought or built their own aircraft and flew them for love or money. While naval and military departments were almost everywhere slow to realise the possibilities of flying, most of them had set up departments of military aviation. Some countries were more enthusiastic and farsighted than others, but on the whole it is fair to say that none of them fully realised the great part that aviation was to play in the wars of the future.

Right: *A morbid view of the 'romance of flying' — German cartoon comments on the high incidence of accidents among the first generation of aviators: 'I must marry an aviator,' reflects the girl enthusiastically. 'Black suits me so well!'*

Chapter 3
Aircraft Go to War

The outbreak of the First World War in 1914 came suddenly, at the time of the August bank holiday in Britain, and when most people in Europe were about to begin their summer vacations. But though the suddenness of war startled the peoples of Europe, it came as no surprise to most governments. Its possibility had long been foreseen, and plans for mobilisation and for the opening moves had been drawn up and were ready to be put into effect. Once again was heard the ominous tramp of armies going to battle. But this time there was a new sound – the whine and drone of an occasional aeroplane overhead. Few could have foreseen that within four years that drone would have been amplified to the tremendous roar of great fleets of aircraft, a roar so mighty that at times it almost overwhelmed the crash of artillery and the sinister rattle of small arms fire.

At the outbreak of war the RFC went to the Continent with the British Expeditionary Force. Indeed, it preceded the BEF, owing to its remarkable mobility. It consisted of a headquarters, four aeroplane squadrons, some observation balloons, and an aircraft park for general repair work: a total of 105 officers and about 500 men. Two of the squadrons had a wireless flight to explore the possibilities of radio communications between air and ground.

The size of the air contingents of the other belligerent powers was comparable, except for Russia which seems at this stage to have mobilised no effective units of military aviation. The French, in spite of their uncertainty as to the employment of aircraft in war, probably had the largest contingent, consisting of some 250 assorted aeroplanes.

The infantry divisions marched to war, and almost all their guns and transport were horse-drawn. They relied on cavalry to scout ahead of them, to make contact with the enemy and send back information as to his strength and dispositions. From these reports the intelligence staffs attempted to assess the order of battle and the intentions of the opposing forces. Such information was often woe-

Left: Poised to attack – Albatros DIIIs of the German air force

fully incomplete and sometimes incorrect but apart from a few agents' reports – frequently unreliable and usually out of date – it was all that they had to go upon. It was clearly a matter of great importance to supplement this information in any way possible, and the most promising way of doing so seemed to be by observation from the air.

However, military leaders in many countries were inclined to be sceptical about the value of air reconnaissance. Few of them, if any, had flown personally, and they found it difficult to realise how much, or how little, could be seen from the air. Not all previous experience had been encouraging from the point of view of the higher command. General Sir Ian Hamilton, attached to the Japanese army during the Russo-Japanese War in 1904, noted in his diary 'the Russians are sending up balloons to our front, and in front of the Twelfth Division. Judging by manoeuvres and South African experiences, they should now obtain a lot of misleading intelligence.' It was often pointed out that observers from the air, unlike cavalry patrols, could not identify enemy units or take prisoners for interrogation. However, although there was not a great deal of confidence in air reconnaissance, there was no other apparent use for military aviation, and such war flights as were made during the first few weeks of hostilities had some form of reconnaissance as their object.

The British provided an exception to this generally vague attitude. They had from the beginning a perfectly clear, if somewhat limited, idea of what they expected from military aviation. It was to be reconnaissance, nothing more nor less, and pilots and observers were trained with this end in view. Of course, there were varying degrees of enthusiasm, or lack of it, among the military authorities, but by and large the General Staff, taking into consideration all previous experience, hoped that aircraft would be able to fly over the enemy's rear areas, and report on troop concentrations, traffic density on road and rail, and the location of dumps and depots. This information, added to that obtained from cavalry patrols and agents, would greatly help the intelligence staff to solve its difficult problems. The admirals hoped that aircraft could rapidly survey vast areas of sea, and keep an eye on the whereabouts of the enemy's main fleets. Thus Royal Navy vessels could avoid, or perhaps themselves achieve, surprise, and the risk of being caught at a tactical disadvantage at sea would be much reduced. Air reconnaissance at sea is more complete and positive than air reconnaissance over land. No vessel, other than

Right: Increase of air strength on the Western Front, 1914-18.
Far right: Representative British types, 1912-17: an impressive improvement in performance and armament under the spur of war

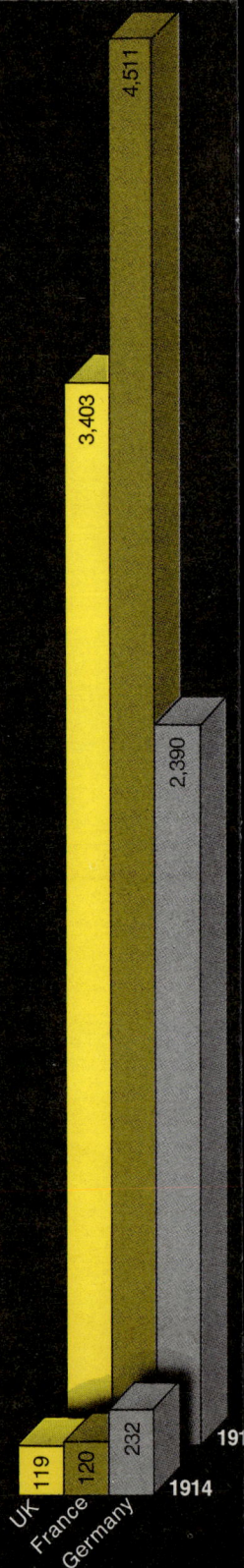

4,511

3,403

2,390

232

UK 119

France 120

Germany 232

1914

191

1912
BE2 One 100lb bomb;
hand grenades, rifle, and
pistols carried by pilot

70hp   70mph *

1915
DH2 One Lewis machine gun

100hp   93mph *

1916
Sopwith Pup One Vickers
machine gun,
four 25lb bombs

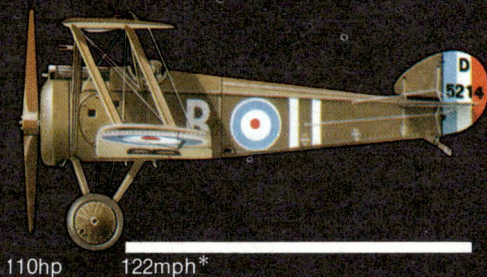

80hp   115mph *

1917
Sopwith Camel Two
synchronised Vickers
machine guns,
four 25lb bombs

110hp   122mph *

1917
Se5a One Vickers machine
gun, one Lewis machine gun,
four 25lb bombs

240hp   135mph *

*Maximum at ground level

a submarine, can escape observation unless there is a dense fog, and it can be more certainly identified by those who understand their business than can a military formation or unit. And Britain, not only in those days a great sea power but also, then as now, dependent on sea transport for her vital imports of food, oil, and raw materials, had a very special interest in air/sea reconnaissance. There was thus a good reason for this attitude towards air reconnaissance, especially on the part of the Admiralty.

Effects of wartime reconnaissance

The Italians, also encouraged by their former experiences, were inclined to hope for many benefits from air reconnaissance, but the French were more cautious in their attitude. The German navy had considerable faith in its Zeppelins, but very early in the war an incident occurred which did much to shake the confidence of the German army in the value of aircraft in reconnaissance. In the opening campaign of the war, General Alexander von Kluck, commanding the 1st Army on the right flank of the German advance on Paris, soon found himself in difficulty. Although after the first encounter the British and French forces were in retreat, it was a retreat in good order and not a rout. In vain von Kluck moved north and west in an endeavour to outflank the British army on the Allies' left wing. It became for him a matter of supreme importance to know the line of the British retreat, for in his efforts to outflank them he had opened a wide and potentially dangerous gap between himself and von Bülow's 2nd Army on his left. Although von Kluck had not much faith in air reconnaissance he attempted to use it — *faute de mieux*.

At length he received a report which seemed to him to be of value. Perhaps he relied on it more than on most because the observer had a connection with his family and the message was what he wanted to hear. The report read: 'All roads through the Forêt de Mormal clear of troops.' This was, to von Kluck, good news. He took it to mean that the British retreat was taking a more southerly course, and that he had a good chance of outflanking them. So he pressed on, disregarding the gap. But his manoeuvre failed. The gap which he had rather recklessly ignored was exploited by the French. General Gallieni's famous 'taxi-cab army', making a sortie from the environs of Paris in commandeered motor vehicles, found the gap and the threat brought the German advance to a halt. The battles of the Marne and Aisne forced them to retreat, and both sides, in order to secure their flanks, began the race northwards to the coast. The German plan had failed and a stalemate that was to last with slight modifications for more than three years set in. And in this failure von

Kluck's reliance on a misleading air reconnaissance report had played a significant part.

What had happened was this. The British troops were well-trained and at the approach of any aeroplane – none could tell whether it was friend or foe – they took cover. Where roads ran through a forest this was easy; it took but a few moments for men, horses, guns, and transport to halt and move off the road under the shelter of the trees. The observer in the aircraft then saw nothing and reported the roads clear. Thus was learned the first and perhaps the most important lesson of air reconnaissance; positive sighting of anything from the air was valuable, but negative information could be very misleading. It did not follow that because an observer saw nothing there was nothing there.

Unhappily this incident and other less fateful ones did not increase confidence in the value of air reconnaissance. Inexperienced observers made mistakes, as was but natural. But on the other hand some valuable information was gained. For example, the British Commander-in-Chief, Sir John French, first became fully aware of the German attempt at envelopment when an aircraft reported a long column moving westwards along the Brussels-Ninove road. This was confirmed when another air reconnaissance reported enemy troops moving in force along a road leading to Soignies, although the Germans were using the trees bordering the road in an attempt to conceal their movements.

On 22nd August a British aeroplane failed to return from a reconnaissance mission, and it was probable that it was shot down by fire from the ground. It is an interesting commentary on the general lack of information – the fog of war – that the capture of this aeroplane provided the first confirmation that von Kluck had of the presence of the British Expeditionary Force on the Continent.

On the Eastern Front the Germans made quite good use of their aircraft to keep track of the Russian advance which was two-pronged. Ludendorff's plan was to concentrate the whole of his force against one prong which was all but annihilated at the battle of Tannenberg. He then made use of the excellent lateral rail communications to move his whole force to deal with the other prong which was destroyed in the battle of the Masurian Lakes. If the Russians had possessed any military aviation trained in air reconnaissance and had used it properly they might have avoided the traps set for them. These calamitous defeats, and the suicide of one of their chief commanders, General Samsonov, started the demoralisation of the

Left: *Making the machines – Vickers aircraft factory shop floor*

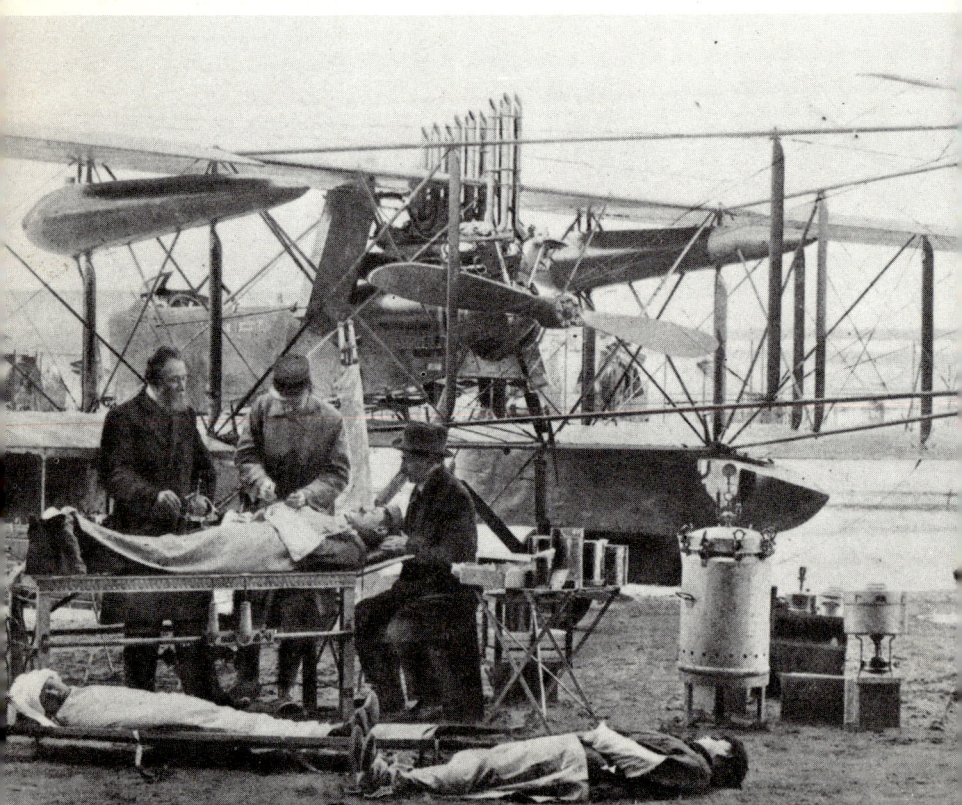

Tsar's armed forces, which led in due course to the Bolshevik Revolution and the military collapse of Russia. The whole subsequent history of Russia, and indeed of Europe, might have been very different if those disasters had been avoided.

It can therefore be seen that even at this early date in the war aircraft had already been involved in critical affairs with far-reaching consequences. It is doubtful, however, if many higher commanders fully realised this, and indeed the French High Command had scant faith in the value of air reconnaissance and took the view that aircraft did little more than add a further complication to the already complex business of war. This was not an attitude which encouraged their military aviators.

The drawbacks of visual reconnaissance were by this time widely recognised, and many of those concerned were giving much thought to improved methods. There were two main lines of approach to the problem. First, it was obvious that if a camera could be used effectively from the air it would provide a permanent and incontrovertible record. Second, if reliable radio communications could be established between air and ground it would mean that news could be transmitted immediately, without waiting for the aircraft to return and land.

Aerial cameras had been produced, but it was only to be expected that they were not yet very successful. There were hard problems to be solved: the relatively high rate of motion of aircraft, the very long focal length, and the manipulation of the camera itself. It was, however, recognised at an early stage that the camera would be a most important aid to air reconnaissance.

Before the war many experiments had been tried in several countries with the use of the new Marconi system of wireless communication to transmit messages from aircraft. In 1912 the French inventor Lucien Rouzet produced a light-weight transmitter, and some of these were purchased by several countries. In Britain the non-rigid airships *Delta* and *Eta* employed wireless with some success during the army manoeuvres of 1913, and French and German airships had also successfully used radio for messages to and from the ground and in communication from ship to ship. At much the same time two-way messages were exchanged between aeroplanes and the ground, though engine noise often made reception difficult.

It was necessary in those days for aircraft to trail a long copper wire as an aerial, weighted at the end by a plummet of lead which could be let out or wound in by a hand-operated reel under the control of the observer. It was, however, next to impossible for any faults that might

Top left: *Observers survey the front to pinpoint artillery targets.*
Bottom: *French Red Cross air team pose for the cameraman*

arise to be corrected in the air, and so the standard of reliability was not very high. All messages had to be sent by the Morse Code as speech was not yet practicable.

One of the many tribulations suffered by pilots of all the belligerents was the inability of the troops to distinguish between friendly and hostile aircraft. This is a difficulty which has never been fully overcome. A flight commander in one of the British squadrons later remarked that he was sorry to see the arrival of the BEF 'because up till then we had only been fired on by the French whenever we flew. Now we were fired on by French and English . . . . To this day I can remember the roar of musketry that greeted two of our machines as they left the aerodrome and crossed the main Maubeuge-Mons road, along which a British column was proceeding.'

At this time no aircraft carried any national markings, but it was becoming exceedingly obvious that something of the kind was necessary. The British painted a Union Jack on the underside of the wings, but this did not prove to be very easily recognisable and before long the familiar roundels (red upon white upon blue) were adopted. Other nations also adopted distinctive markings—the Iron Cross in black for the Germans, and roundels for the French (blue upon white upon red).

With the stabilising of the war in the West and the construction of elaborate earth-works facing each other at close quarters from the Channel coast to the Swiss frontier, a long drawn-out battle of attrition began. The object was not so much to gain ground as to wear down the other side by a steady erosion of men and materials. Strategically-speaking, such a policy was bankrupt, but it encouraged all kinds of tactical ingenuity. Gradually both sides built up large forces of artillery behind their front lines, and a regular routine of bombardment began. The main targets were enemy batteries (counter-battery work), brigade and battalion headquarters, and communication trenches. In general, the front line trenches were too close to each other—sometimes separated by less than a hundred yards—to offer suitable targets for artillery fire. The longer-range guns, of which at first there were not many, would engage the headquarters of higher formations, ammunition dumps, railheads, and supply distribution centres. It was quickly discovered that aircraft could spot the fall of shells with remarkable precision, and with suitable air to ground communications could correct the fire of batteries so as to engage pin-point targets with great accuracy. This discovery not only opened up a new demand for the services of aircraft, but also stimulated the development of aircraft wireless equipment.

Right: *Italian airmen drop propaganda items upon the enemy*

By the end of 1914 aeroplanes were carrying out a daily routine of reconnaissance and control of artillery fire. The reliability of air to ground wireless steadily improved, and almost all army cooperation aircraft were equipped with it. Captive balloons, which could use telephones, were also used to supplement this work, but they were not so effective as aeroplanes as they had to be stationed well behind the lines for protection from artillery fire. The balloon observers were equipped at an early date with parachutes. These were of the static kind, connected to the balloon basket by a cord; when the wearer jumped the cord was drawn tight and the parachute opened.

Although suitable parachutes were available, they were not generally carried in aeroplanes. The reasons for this are not entirely clear, but it seems that the military authorities took the view that pilots and observers might be tempted to abandon their aircraft unnecessarily. It was still believed that the gun, weapon, or machine was more important than the man — a view that is very rightly no longer held.

It was not long before methods of anti-aircraft (AA) artillery fire were developed. Germany had already given some attention to this problem, and in 1910 Krupps had produced three prototype AA guns: the 65 mm (9 lb shell), the 75 mm (12 lb) and a much larger weapon, the 105 mm (40 lb). The Germans actually had thirty-six AA guns, mostly of the smaller kind, at the outbreak of the war. The French may have had a few of their famous 75 mm guns adapted for AA fire, but the British had none. As a temporary measure, a number of field guns were mounted (lowering the trails by digging in) so as to fire at a high angle. But whether specially-designed or improvised AA guns were used, the control system was primitive and the shooting very far from accurate.

Naval demands

The nature of the war at sea was very different from that on land. Naval expansion was not so drastic because warships take a long time to build, and some of the older ones were sunk or became obsolete. In spite of frenzied efforts on the part of the Germans to build up their fleet, the supremacy at sea of the Allies was very marked, and they were eager to take the offensive. But unlike an army, a fleet can — if it does not wish to fight — withdraw itself into the safety of well-defended bases and anchorages. In this secure position it can adopt the policy of the 'fleet in being'; the very fact of its existence compels the enemy fleet to maintain a continuous watch on it. The German plan was to tie down the Allied fleets in a watching rôle, while preying upon the Allied sea-borne commerce by means of fast surface raiders, mainly light cruisers,

armed merchant vessels, and submarines. They relied on their fleet of Zeppelin airships to enable them to seize the opportunities for these sorties and to steer clear of the periodical sweeps made by the Allied fleets. This policy of raiding is traditional for a weaker sea power.

The Allies expected their naval aircraft to keep track of surface raiders and, as far as possible, of submarines, which, if not too deeply submerged, are visible from the air. If the whereabouts of these vessels were known, merchant shipping could be routed to give them a wide berth and opportunities provided for patrolling warships to find and destroy them.

For reconnaissance at sea a long range was of great value, but speed of less importance. The demand for artillery spotting and photography was negligible, but wireless telegraphy for the rapid transmission of news over long distances was an urgent necessity. From the outset, therefore, the operational requirements for naval aircraft differed from those of aircraft engaged in army co-operation duties. The work of naval observers was also widely different from that required over land, and their training therefore showed a marked divergence.

The fact that the tasks of naval aviation were so different from those of army cooperation aircraft and the well-known aloofness and self-sufficiency of navies the world over were the main causes of the separation and lack of cooperation between naval and military air services. There is no doubt that for these reasons there was in France, Germany, and the United States, as well as in Britain, a marked lack of sympathy and understanding between the naval and military wings.

It was understandable that navies should be more interested in airships than were armies, but they also tended to adopt different methods of aircraft procurement. In Britain this was peculiarly marked, and needs some explanation. The Royal Navy was used to dealing with private firms for the building of warships and for the provision of guns and other equipment. The Admiralty therefore turned naturally to private firms for the supply of aeroplanes. On the other hand, the Army was more used to dealing with ordnance factories, and had relatively little experience of dealing with, or knowledge of, private firms. It therefore naturally relied on the Royal Aircraft Factory at Farnborough, which was in practice an ordnance factory, to supply its needs. It is true that the Admiralty made good use of the research work carried out at Farnborough, and it was perhaps a difference of attitude rather than of deliberate policy. But while the Army relied heavily on the Factory, the Admiralty had as

Left: German photographic observation from a captive balloon

few dealings with it as possible. The result of this was that while the aircraft of the Army, though sound, were rather mediocre and unenterprising, naval aircraft tended to be more varied and interesting.

As early as 1911 various experiments had been made in operating aircraft on the water. The pioneer of this development in Britain was the famous firm of Short Brothers. The first idea was to launch an aeroplane from a ship by means of a trackway, and allow it to alight on the sea by means of an undercarriage fitted with air bags. Though successful, this was not very satisfactory, and some form of flotation gear which would enable the aircraft to take off from the water was required. A design of floats was eventually worked out which achieved this, and the seaplane was successfully flown by Lieutenant C. R. Samson RN.

Many countries were experimenting with flying-boats, notably Curtiss in America and Sopwith in Britain. In these aircraft the fuselage was built in the form of a hard-chine boat, capable of taking off from, riding upon, and alighting on water.

The Royal Navy also used a simple type of small non-rigid airship, known affectionately as the 'Blimp'. This was designed by the Royal Aircraft Factory at Farnborough, and consisted of a streamlined envelope from which was suspended a BE2C aeroplane fuselage. It was powered by a 90 hp air-cooled engine of Factory design, which had been produced in large numbers for the whole range of BE2 aircraft. These little ships proved most effective for coastal patrol work, escorting convoys, and searching for German U-boats. They were relatively easy to handle and had other advantages over aeroplanes, including very long endurance and ability to fly at slow speeds when on escort duties. Their main disadvantage was the unsatisfactory accommodation for the crew of two, who were confined for long periods in cramped and exposed aeroplane cockpits. A few large rigid airships were later built and used successfully for long distance sea reconnaissance.

The Allied navies were much concerned at the possible activities of the German Zeppelins, whose long range gave them great advantages for maritime reconnaissance. It was realised that these giant airships, with envelopes filled with hydrogen gas, were potentially vulnerable to incendiary attack. In October 1913 Winston Churchill, then First Lord of the Admiralty, foresaw the probable rôle of the Zeppelins in war and wrote a minute in which he suggested various ways of dealing with them. They

*Top left: German marine airship L31 on a reconnaissance mission. **Bottom:** The British seaplane carrier HMS* Engadine

should be attacked, he believed, from above by discharging a string of fire-balls, which 'would be drawn like a whiplash across the envelope'. Alternatively a series of small bombs, with fuses sensitive enough to detonate on striking the rubberised cotton fabric of the Zeppelin's envelope, could be used, or a Hales grenade fired from a service rifle. For the more distant future the bombing of Zeppelin sheds from the air was envisaged.

At the beginning of the war the only weapon actually available for attacking Zeppelins in the air was the Hales grenade, which had been fitted with an especially sensitive fuse after experiments carried out at the Royal Aircraft Factory at Farnborough.

By the end of 1914 all the belligerent nations, with the exception of Russia, had put in hand a very large expansion of their military and naval air services. Though their ideas were strictly limited, higher commands everywhere were beginning to realise the important contribution that aircraft could make to the conduct of warfare. Much thought had been given to the future by the enthusiasts. Many new and sometimes startling ideas had been explored, and much experimental work had been started. All concerned in these developments believed that they were on the brink of great advances.

Top right: German aircraft is drawn in sections by horses towards the front. **Bottom:** British Bristol Scout aircraft

Chapter 4
Air Combat

It had been believed before the war that reconnaissance could be effectively carried out only from a low height, that is to say at about 1,500 feet or even less, and that in any event the frequent presence of cloud would necessitate low flying in order to see the ground. It was thought that owing to their relatively high speeds aeroplanes would have little to fear from small arms or artillery fire. It was soon found, however, that this was not so, and pilots were forced to fly higher. To everyone's surprise it was discovered that reconnaissance, given reasonable visibility, could be carried out at much greater heights. Observations of rail and road traffic could be successfully undertaken at heights of 10,000 feet or more.

It had long been a military maxim that information must be fought for, and this was certainly true so long as warfare was confined to two dimensions. Cavalry patrols or advance guards had to make contact with the enemy in order to force him to reveal his strength and dispositions, and to capture prisoners for the identification of units and for questioning by the intelligence staffs. With the coming of aircraft war had expanded into three dimensions, and it seemed that this maxim was no longer valid. The ocean of the air, covering both land and sea, provided a medium through which aircraft could pass at will. Defences and obstacles could be used to prevent the passage of land or sea forces, but no fortifications or obstacles served to bar the movement of aircraft, which could fly over land and sea, and over enemy as well as friendly territories. Except, therefore, when flying low, aeroplanes proved to be largely invulnerable and could gain information without having to fight for it.

Before long every army corps was demanding more and more reconnaissance and artillery spotting and, on the Western Front at least, wanted at least one aeroplane squadron and several balloons under its exclusive control for these routine tasks.

As the number of aircraft over the front lines gradually grew, encounters in the air became more numerous. 58 ▷

Left: Italian aircraft destroys Drachen tethered kite balloon

Aircraft of the First World War

British: 1 The De Havilland 2 fighter, brought into service in 1916. **2** The excellent daylight bomber DH4. **3** Credited with shooting down more enemy aircraft than any other type, the famous Sopwith Camel. **4** Another speedy and reliable fighter, the SE5a. **French: 5** The Nieuport 11, one of the most successful fighter aircraft, employed by the air forces of Britain, Russia, and Belgium as well as France. **6** The Spad 16 — in the photograph is the Spad used by the American general 'Billy' Mitchell. A number of American units were equipped with Spad machines. **German: 7** Naval airship L9 at the Friedrichshaven base. **8** Fokker EI — fitted with the synchronising gear, this aeroplane wrought havoc among Allied craft in 1915 and 1916, earning the title 'Fokker scourge': **Below:** The Fokker Dr I *(Dreidecker),* inspired by the highly successful British Sopwith Triplane. It was the favourite aircraft of a number of German air aces, including Werner Voss and Manfred von Richthofen

2

4

6

8

Soldiers are trained to fight and it was frustrating for them to realise that aeroplanes were unable to engage each other in combat. In an effort to overcome this, some observers began to carry rifles into the air and took pot-shots at an enemy aircraft whenever an opportunity offered. It was soon apparent that rifles were uncommonly awkward things to handle, even in a relatively slow slip-stream of 60-70 mph. After much unsuccessful effort they were discarded in favour of revolvers and automatic pistols. These did not, however, prove to be much more effective, because aircraft in motion are peculiarly diffi-cult targets for such weapons, and it was rare indeed for any hits to be scored. The only other way of damaging a hostile aircraft was to ram it. Though this was done on occasions, it was a practice which, for reasons that are readily understandable, never became popular.

All the belligerent air forces were experimenting with various methods of mounting machine-guns in aircraft. Only the lighter, air-cooled types could, of course, be carried, and even these were liable when fired in the air to cause damage to structures not designed to with-stand the shock and vibration caused by their discharge. As far as Britain was concerned, it is interesting to note that the RNAS had given more thought to this problem than had the RFC. It seems paradoxical that the force which had less contact with the enemy should have de-voted more attention to offensive measures. No doubt the reason for this was to be found in the diverse tasks of the naval and military wings of aviation. The military wings had proved to be far too small for their ever-increasing tasks and they had to expand as rapidly as possible, but their main duty was army cooperation which absorbed all their resources. They had not much spare time and energy to devote to seeking battle in the air. The naval service, on the other hand, was not so ex-tended and had more chance to think of such things as air-gunnery and bomb-dropping.

The demand for long-range reconnaissance over land had produced a variety of faster aeroplanes, mostly small single-seaters such as the German Fokker and French Morane monoplanes, and the French Nieuport Bébé and British Bristol Scout biplanes. These aircraft were called 'scouts', because they were designed for the task of pene-trating far over enemy territory to observe – and some-times to photograph – the build-up of depots, dumps, and concentrations of troops in reserve.

Top, left: Pilot and tail-gunner of an observation aircraft.
Bottom: German aircrew. Early attempts at mounting a machine gun had the gunners firing from the nose of the aeroplane over the head of the pilot. Top, right: Crew of British FE2d

It is not surprising that many pilots were attracted by the idea of mounting a machine-gun in these small fast aircraft, and thus turning them into fighters. It was soon obvious that the most, perhaps the only, satisfactory mounting was one which enabled a fixed machine-gun to be fired straight ahead in the line of flight. This ideal arrangement was difficult to achieve. If the gun was mounted in or near the cockpit, so as to be under the pilot's control, it could not fire dead ahead because of the obstruction caused by the airscrew. If, on the other hand, it was mounted on or above the wing, so as to fire clear of the revolving airscrew, it could not be reloaded and the drums or clips held at the most less than fifty rounds of ammunition. This represented only a few seconds' fire. In addition, jamming, which was very frequent in those days, could not be cleared. As a compromise guns could be mounted close to the cockpit so as to fire obliquely forward to one side or other of the airscrew. This was a clumsy arrangement involving deflection shots and consequent difficulties in aiming. Some success was, however, achieved in this way. Captain L. G. Hawker, a gallant and ingenious Royal Engineer officer attached to the RFC as a pilot, succeeded in shooting down three German aircraft in the course of one patrol with a machine-gun mounted in this way. For this remarkable exploit he was awarded the Victoria Cross.

In all the belligerent air forces a few pilots using this kind of mounting managed to shoot down enemy aircraft on rare occasions, and so did a few observers who had rigged up machine-gun mountings in their cockpits. But although encounters between aircraft were not rare, and were becoming less so, it was seldom indeed that they resulted in an enemy aircraft being shot down.

The Germans had armed a number of their big, heavy two-seater army cooperation aircraft with a machine-gun under the control of the observer. This was intended to be a defensive measure, but the more aggressive aircrews set about devising tactics whereby the observer's gun could be used for attack. This was difficult and met with no general success, but the future famous ace Oswold Boelcke, with Lieutenant von Wuelisch as observer, managed to shoot down a French Morane monoplane. Max Immelmann, another future ace, with von Teubern as observer, also had some success, but it was clear that no great results would be achieved until the problem of firing a machine-gun dead ahead in the line of flight had been solved. The will to fight was there, but the means of doing so effectively were not yet to hand.

Left: Early in the war, a primitive anti-aircraft device—French front-line troops mount a Hotchkiss machine gun on a wheel

The first step towards solving this problem was taken by the French. Roland Garros, a veteran pilot who had learned to fly some years before the war and who was well-known as a pioneer of long-distance and exhibition flying, had an idea for permitting a machine-gun to be fired through a revolving airscrew. The plan was simple: a machine-gun was mounted in the cockpit of a Morane monoplane and lined up to fire straight ahead. Steel wedges were bolted to each airscrew blade, in such a way as to act as deflectors in the event of a bullet striking them. It was estimated that no more than ten per cent of the bullets would strike the deflectors, leaving ninety per cent for the destruction of the target.

This simple arrangement, though not entirely satisfactory, inaugurated a new era. The single-seater fighter, with a fixed gun firing forward which could be aimed by the pilot flying his machine so as to bring the sights to bear on the target, had arrived. During the first half of April 1915 Garros shot down several enemy aircraft, and the French, seeing that the device was successful, decided to equip all their Morane monoplanes with these deflectors. On 18th April, however, Garros himself was shot down on the German side of the lines while bombing a train from a low height. His engine had been hit and put out of action. He made a successful forced landing and attempted to set fire to his aircraft. He was quickly captured, and unfortunately the aeroplane did not burn well enough to destroy the deflector plates. The Germans realised their import, and decided to equip their Fokker M5 monoplane with a similar device.

The designer, Anthony Fokker, was not enthusiastic about the idea. He realised that the deflected bullets might go anywhere: they might damage the engine, might place additional stresses on the airscrew blades which could lead to their disintegration with disastrous results, might even cause danger to neighbouring friendly aircraft. In his view the correct solution was to regulate the firing of the gun so that the bullets were bound to pass between the airscrew blades. The way to do this, he believed, was to make the airscrew itself fire the gun. Cams on the airscrew hub could be made by means of a direct mechanical linkage to fire the gun at the correct moment.

Now at last the aeroplane had acquired true tactical offensive power, capable of shooting down other aeroplanes, and of attacking balloons, airships, and targets on the ground. The best German pilots were given the new modified Fokker E1 and soon began to amass a large total of enemy aircraft destroyed.

Right: A more sophisticated and effective means of dealing with the menace from the sky—a mobile German anti-aircraft unit

Foremost among these were Udet, Immelmann, and
Boelcke. Ernst Udet was a pleasant, easy-going youth
who, though high-spirited and adventurous, was re-
luctant to kill. He made a resolute effort to overcome this,
and became one of the most successful German pilots.
Immelmann was famous as a tactician and invented
several combat manoeuvres, one of which—the Immelmann turn—is known by that name to this day. Boelcke,
quiet and methodical, had a reputation for fairness and
generosity as well as courage. Immelmann and Boelcke
were killed in battle, but Udet survived to become a
general and, alas, to commit suicide in despair at the
excesses of Hitler's government. All three men inspired
affection in their comrades and respect in their enemies.
And with the tremendous advantage given the German
air force by Anthony Fokker's invention, they and their
colleagues soon won a large measure of control of the
air over the whole of the Western Front.

The Germans, conscious of the importance of this interruptor gear, issued orders that no E type Fokker should
venture beyond the front line. It was, however, soon clear
to the Allies that the Germans possessed some device
which had effectively solved the problem of firing a gun
through a revolving airscrew. Apart from the use of
deflector plates, which were not proving very satisfactory,
the immediate Allied answer was to fit a Lewis gun on the
top wing of small, fast biplanes such as the Nieuport Bébé
and the Bristol Scout. This had three disadvantages. First,
the line of sight and the line of fire of the gun were
several feet apart, and converged only at one definite
range. This caused a serious tactical restriction in aerial
combat. Second, the drum of the Lewis gun contained only
forty-seven rounds or about five seconds' fire, which com-
pared very badly with the Fokker's belt-fed gun with some
400 rounds. Finally, the gun in the Fokker was in the
pilot's cockpit, and he was therefore able to take the
necessary action to clear jams, while a gun on the top
wing was out of reach, and if it jammed could not be
re-started.

Nevertheless, a number of French and British pilots
acquired great skill in shooting down enemy aircraft
with the expenditure of very little ammunition. Navarre,
for example, is credited with having shot down some of his
victims with as few as half-a-dozen rounds. This was
usually achieved by stalking an enemy from a blind
spot, generally from below and behind, then pulling up
the nose of the aircraft to fire a short burst at close range.

The Allies realised, however, that if the Germans' air
superiority was to be reduced or eliminated some better
method, which would not need exceptional expertise,
must be devised. German fighter activity was seriously

⁵ interfering with the routine of army cooperation duties, and was causing an unacceptably high rate of casualties. Allied military aviation was prevented from giving the armies the assistance that they now regarded as essential, and the high casualty rate was crippling military aviation's plans for expansion.

The end of Fokker supremacy

Aircraft at this stage of their development were relatively small and of simple construction, mainly of wood with wire bracing. It did not, therefore, take very long to bring a new design into service in reasonable numbers – possibly a year or even less. Engines might take rather longer to develop and produce, but a good standard engine could be used to power many different kinds of aircraft. The British had decided that their answer to the problem of firing a gun straight ahead in the line of flight would be the 'pusher' biplane. In this type of aircraft the engine and propeller were placed behind the pilot at the after end of a short nacelle. The rear part of the fuselage was replaced by a pair of tail-booms supporting the tail-plane and rudder. Not only did this arrangement provide a gun able to fire straight ahead, but it gave the pilot an unrestricted view far superior to any that could be provided by the normal tractor type aircraft. If to these advantages could be added good performance and manoeuvrability, an almost ideal fighting machine would result.

The DH2, a small fast pusher biplane designed and produced by the De Havilland Company, proved to combine all these advantages. By the spring of 1916 it was being produced in quantity, and provided the standard fighter for the RFC. The French Nieuport Bébé, in the hands of expert French pilots, was also proving to be a very effective fighter. Neither of these aircraft was faster or better armed than the Fokker or Pfalz, though the modification of the drum for the Lewis gun to hold ninety-eight rounds was an improvement. Since they were biplanes, however, they were more buoyant at high altitudes, stronger in their construction, and very much more manoeuvrable.

At about this time an important change in the organisation of fighter aircraft occurred. Hitherto they had been dispersed in small numbers, two or three being attached to each army cooperation squadron, and their task was to give such protection as they could to the aircraft of their own squadron. This arrangement was becoming ineffective and uneconomical, and the fighters were withdrawn

Left: The aces –German: 1 Ernst Udet. 2 Oswald Boelcke. 3 Max Immelmann. 4 von Richthofen. French: 5 Jean Navarre. 6 René Fonck. British: 7 L.G.Hawker. Canadian: 8 W.A.Bishop

65

and concentrated into fighter squadrons. This concentration into one unit of aircraft of the same type led to the practice of flying in formation, at first in twos or threes and later as many as six. Larger formations than this were found to be unmanageable.

The success of the E type Fokker, followed by that of the French and British fighters, made it necessary to provide the army cooperation two-seaters with effective defensive armaments. It had been the general practice in these aircraft to place the pilot in the rear seat and the observer in the front seat. It was difficult, if not impossible, in these circumstances to provide an efficient gun-mounting for the observer. When attacked from astern, which was the usual method, he had to fire backwards over the pilot's head, and this and the centre-section struts severely limited his field of fire. So the pilot and observer changed places; with the pilot in front the observer had a vastly improved range of vision and field of fire. Better gun mountings, notably the British Scarff ring, came into service, and from then on the two-seater had a reasonable chance of defending itself against fighter attacks. The British also produced a very useful two-seater pusher biplane in the form of the FE2b, designed for army cooperation duties.

A general pattern of tactics now began to emerge. The army cooperation aircraft flew to and fro over or near the front lines, going about their routine business while the fighter patrols, now often consisting of formations of from three to six aircraft, flew above and beyond them. In theory if any fighters attempted to attack the army cooperation aircraft they would be engaged and a fighter battle would ensue. In practice, the number of fighters available was as yet too small to provide a complete cover. This provided opportunities for enemy fighters to slip through and attack the army cooperation aircraft.

The impossibility of providing adequate security for the army cooperation aircraft by means of fighter patrols along the front gave rise to the doctrine of air superiority of which General Sir Hugh Trenchard, commanding the RFC on the Western Front, was a strong protagonist. This doctrine maintained that it was not sufficient for fighter patrols to attempt to defend the army cooperation aircraft from attack; they should take the offensive, seek out the enemy fighter patrols, and destroy them. By so doing, they would force the enemy to adopt a defensive rôle. His fighter patrols would be forced further back from the front line and their opportunities for attacking army cooperation aircraft would be much reduced.

Left: Milan magazine salutes Italy's aviators — in most warring states the air aces quickly became great national heroes

This new doctrine of offensive patrols was adopted whole-heartedly by the RFC, and with only slightly less enthusiasm by the French. The Germans did not need to adopt it as their defensive fighter cover was sufficient during the limited periods when it was required. This aggressive policy paid off and gained for the Allies a large measure of air superiority. In the late spring and summer of 1916 this ascendancy was possibly greater than that achieved by either side at any other stage in the war. The change had been swift and complete; in less than a year the control of the air had passed from German into Allied hands, and routine German army cooperation work was reduced to a low level. It could not fail to be realised that this was due to the introduction of new and improved fighter aircraft and a new and more aggressive tactical doctrine.

Long range reconnaissance was by now almost entirely photographic and aircraft engaged in these tasks had to be escorted by fighters. The old adage was once more true — information had to be fought for. Escorts never proved very satisfactory because the fighter, though strategically defensive, can achieve its object only by a vigorous tactical offensive. If, therefore, an attack was made on either the reconnaissance aircraft or its escort the only thing that the escorting fighters could do was to attack the enemy fighters. At once a mêlée would ensue with fighters circling round, each trying to get into a position to bring its forward-firing gun to bear. This 'dog-fight', as it was called, would draw the fighters away from the recon-naissance aircraft that they were supposed to protect and leave it open to attack by another wave of enemy fighters. This problem was never satisfactorily solved, but as an alternative a single photographic aircraft would be sent over at a great height in clear weather, relying for safety on evasion.

Superimposed on this general tactical system was a new development. In all the air forces a limited number of exceptionally successful fighter pilots emerged. They owed their success to their unusual skill in marksmanship and piloting, and to a highly aggressive spirit combined with a cool head and steady nerves. Their technique was to spot an enemy aircraft and then to stalk it with great care, usually trying to approach it from a blind spot. Then, at very short range, they would fire a short burst of very accurately aimed fire and break off the fight. These 'lone-hunters' usually did little routine patrolling in formation but were allowed to operate as and when they pleased. Many of them were extremely successful.

Right: Dog-fight between Allied and German planes — the artist C.R.W.Nevinson depicts the strange beauty of aerial combat

The well-known British pilot Albert Ball was the pioneer of these 'lone-hunters'. A quiet, mechanically-minded young man, he was nothing like the reckless, dare-devil popular image of an air ace. After a most successful career he vanished during a dog-fight one day in May 1917. No one knows how he met his end. James McCudden, A. W. Beauchamp-Proctor, and the great French ace René Fonck followed in his footsteps, and all three amassed large scores of enemy aircraft destroyed.

By the end of 1916 the Germans were bringing into service their new fighters to replace the now obsolete Fokker and Pfalz monoplanes. Prominent among these were the early marks of Albatros biplane and the new Pfalz biplane, all with twin forward-firing guns fitted with interruptor gears. Once again the tables were turned and by the spring of 1917 the German air force had regained its former ascendancy. The DH2, with its later counterpart the FE8 built by the Royal Aircraft Factory at Farnborough, and the Nieuport Bébé were outclassed and had become obsolete. So seriously did the Allied situation deteriorate that April 1917 was known in the RFC as 'Bloody April', on account of the very heavy rate of casualties incurred in its efforts to continue, at all costs, to carry out routine tasks and patrols. Once again the importance of technical superiority was demonstrated in a wholly unmistakable manner.

This German ascendancy did not, however, last very long. The Allies had foreseen the inevitable obsolescence of their existing fighters and during the summer they brought into service a number of new fast fighters, equipped with twin belt-fed guns and a mechanical interruptor gear – the Constantinesco. The most successful of these new aircraft were the French Spad and Nieuport 17, and the British Sopwith Camel and the Farnborough-built SE5a.

Rival formations

By this time the organisation and tactics of the belligerent air forces had begun to acquire well-defined national characteristics. It will be convenient to deal first with the British. The RFC was organised into four brigades, each of which was allotted to one of the four armies on the Western Front. Thus the 1st Brigade, RFC was an integral part of the 1st Army, BEF, and so on. Each brigade consisted of two wings, one of fighters and one of army cooperation aircraft. The latter were still further decentralised by placing one army cooperation squadron under the operational control of each army corps. The whole of the RFC on the Western Front was under a general headquarters which had limited powers. It could not, for example, transfer squadrons from one

brigade to another without the concurrence of the army headquarters concerned. Nor could it interfere with the daily routine of army cooperation or fighter patrols, orders for which were issued by the relevant corps or army. Administrative matters, except for rations and accommodation, were the responsibility of GHQ, RFC.

It will be seen that this organisation was excessively decentralised; the available air forces were evenly spread over the whole of the British front, a distance of some 120 miles. No concentration at a decisive time and place was possible without the concurrence of the army commanders which was in practice seldom if ever forthcoming.

The Germans had adopted a much more centralised, and therefore flexible, system. The whole of their available air power was under the control of the Air Headquarters, and such formations and units as were deemed necessary were placed under the *temporary* operational control of the armies. Air Headquarters was an integral part of the Supreme General Headquarters, and thus had power to concentrate air units at any point along the front where they were most needed. This was an advantage which tended to increase as the war went on.

The French system was neither so rigidly decentralised as the British, nor as centralised as the German. The Grand Quartier-General retained the ability to move and concentrate air units as required, but this power was used rather sparingly for fear of upsetting the army commanders.

The general tactical system also showed distinct divergences along national lines. The British insisted on maintaining the work of the army cooperation squadrons from dawn to dusk in all possible weather conditions. This was no doubt due to the effective operational control that the armies and corps had acquired over all air operations, but it meant that protective fighter patrols had also to be in the air whenever flying was possible during daylight hours. Since numbers were limited some fighters were always present, but never in great strength. While this had its drawbacks, it accustomed the RFC pilots to being outnumbered and encouraged an aggressive spirit.

The Germans confined their army cooperation work to one or two periods each day, and were able to put up fighters in considerable strength to cover these limited periods. The French, when the air situation was favourable, preferred the British system of continuous daylight activity; when it was unfavourable they resorted to the German system of concentration at certain periods. 74 ▷

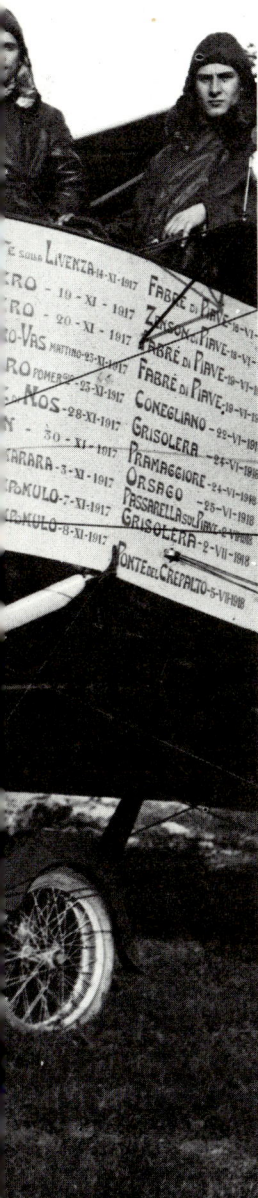

Left: The Italian crew of a Caproni aircraft with their list of victories. *Next page:* A savage dog-fight over the trenches

This was perhaps the most sensible of the three systems.

The German system of centralisation and concentration into periods of intense activity favoured the use of large formations of fighters. These began in a small way when two or three *Jagdstaffeln* (squadrons) were flying together in a loose formation, but gradually increased until whole *Geschwader* (wings) were flying in a co-ordinated manner. This mass was made up of many smaller formations, usually of six or eight aircraft, each under its own leader. During the relatively brief time that these 'circuses', as they were called, were in the air they were very formidable and achieved at least a temporary superiority.

The greatest German formation leader was Manfred von Richthofen, the famous 'Red Baron', so called because his aeroplane was painted scarlet. It was said of him that while he usually shot down his victim, he never lost sight of his own pilots in a mêlée. Whenever one of them got into trouble the Red Baron was at hand to rescue him. But Richthofen had a rather cold and calculating nature, wholly dedicated to air fighting. He had many admirers but few friends. He was killed (exactly how is not known) in April 1918. His aircraft fell behind the British lines.

He was succeeded by Herman Göring, a good pilot and a first-class shot. Jealous of his privileges as a leader, he always took the first shot at an enemy, thus raising his score to a large total. Unlike most other German aces, he was boastful and vainglorious. His subsequent history is well-known.

During the periods of intense activity there were often extensive air battles. As the numbers of fighters available increased, these battles might involve scores of fighters and, towards the end of the war, upwards of a hundred. It might be supposed that these tremendous dog-fights, involving so many aircraft, would result in a very high rate of casualties. This was not so, and after such a mêlée only three or four would probably be lost. The reasons for this were twofold. First, the circumstances permitted only fleeting shots. As soon as a pilot got his sights on an enemy aircraft he would find himself attacked from astern and would have to break off his attack and take evasive action. Aircraft circling round, suddenly appearing and disappearing, seldom gave a chance of a well-aimed, no-deflection shot. Second, even though most fighters had belt-fed twin guns with about 5-600 rounds per gun, this represented only some fifty seconds' fire. Pilots, therefore, especially inexperienced ones, soon ran out of ammunition and had to withdraw from the

Right: *Italian illustration of September 1918—a dire prediction of the shape and power of future aerial Juggernauts*

fight. It was therefore not surprising that the 'lone hunters' notched up a greater score than even the best of the squadron pilots.

During the last years of the war the Allied air effort was boosted by the arrival of the American air force. The United States entered the war too late to have many great aces, but some splendid young Americans, learning to fly at their own expense, had joined one or other of the Allied air forces. Among them was George Vaughn, a typical ace, cool, courageous, and an excellent shot. By the end of the war he had thirteen victories to his credit. Another American, Raoul Lufbery, joined the famous Lafayette French air squadron. He had great success as a lone-hunter, but when the United States entered the war he was switched to teaching young Americans the grim business of air fighting. He was killed in combat in May 1918. Observers saw his body fall away from his burning aeroplane. He had always said that he would never go down in flames. He had kept his word.

1918 was a year of heavy and continuous fighting over the Western Front. It was mostly a 'ding-dong' affair but in the summer, as the war drew towards its close, the German air force began to suffer from shortages of aircraft and equipment. These were due partly to their high rate of wastage but also to the cumulative effects of the Allied sea blockade of Germany. The morale of their fighter pilots began to sag, especially after the failure of the great German March offensive on which they had staked all their hopes. It was the last throw and with its failure the Germans, at least those in the armed forces, began to realise that the war was lost.

The war had seen the birth of the fighter aircraft and its development into a highly formidable weapon. Many thousands of fighter pilots had been trained, and very many had died. For the first time in the history of warfare deadly combat had been lifted into the skies, but the fighter pilots, far above the mud and the blood and the slaughter, had developed a very different attitude from those who fought on the ground. They were almost all young and enthusiastic flyers, untouched by the propaganda of hate disseminated by the belligerent nations. Combat was for them depersonalised; they had no animosity towards their opponents. They fought hard, but often felt pity and even remorse when a vanquished foe was seen to fall in flames. It is no exaggeration to say that they were a gallant band of warriors, unique in modern times, and able to stand comparison with any of the great orders of chivalry of the days of old.

Right: The scourge of the Allied air forces – Baron Manfred von Richthofen (third from left) and fellow German pilots

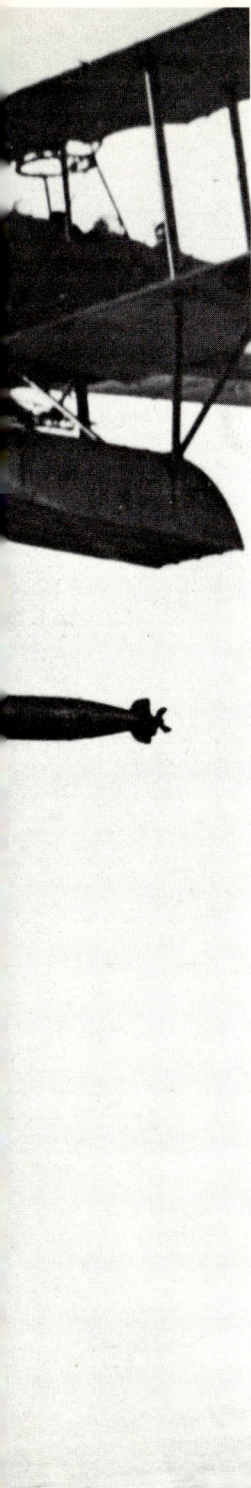

burdened by a daily routine task too big for them, had the time and opportunity to think about the offensive uses of aircraft. The most obvious and promising course of action was to bomb the large sheds in which the Zeppelins were housed. On 22nd September 1914 the RNAS sent four Avro aircraft to bomb the Zeppelin sheds at Dusseldorf. Although some hits were observed, no serious damage was done. A second attack on 8th October was more successful. One aircraft dived down to 600 feet and let go its bombs, some of which scored direct hits. Flames rose to a great height, proving that a Zeppelin had been inside the shed.

In these early attacks the observer had to be left on the ground in order to save weight for bomb carrying and the pilot had, therefore, to navigate as well as fly his aircraft. The absence of any sort of bomb-sight made it necessary to drop bombs from a low height, which brought the aircraft within range of small arms fire from the ground. In addition to those risks, bad weather and unreliable engines made each raid a considerable adventure.

In October the French were contemplating an attack on the Zeppelin base at Friedrichshaven on the north shore of Lake Constance. Here were two airship sheds, one floating on the lake, and an airship and aeroplane factory. It was a most important target. In view, however, of the threat posed by the Zeppelins to British naval supremacy, it was agreed that the RNAS should have the privilege of making the attack but that this should lapse if the raid was not carried out within thirty days. Belfort was chosen as a base, and at the end of October four Avro aircraft in cases, accompanied by pilots, mechanics, and stores, were shipped by night from Southampton to Le Havre, reaching Belfort by rail without incident. The aircraft were erected and tested, and then the pilots waited for suitable weather conditions. At long last, on 21st November, the mists dispersed and the attack took place. Four aircraft were dispatched at five-minute intervals, each carrying four 24 lb bombs. One had difficulty in taking off and was damaged, but the other three reached Friedrichshaven, a distance of some 125 miles, about mid-day and made their attack. Nine bombs fell in the works area, one fell on a shed, seriously damaging a Zeppelin, and the other caused a fire in the gas-works.

All the aircraft encountered heavy fire from the ground and one was hit in the fuel tank and forced to land. The pilot, Squadron Commander E.F. Briggs, was attacked and injured by a crowd of enraged Germans before he was taken into custody and put in a hospital. The other two aircraft returned safely. This flight by the

Left: *Air to sea attack—Short seaplane launches a torpedo*

Avros with their far from reliable 80 hp Gnome engines over some 250 miles of enemy territory was a remarkable exploit. It proved finally that aircraft were capable of offensive action far from the actual battlefield.

The fourth attack took place on Christmas Day 1914. Its target was the Zeppelin base at Cuxhaven, and it differed from the three former attacks in that it was carried out by seaplanes. The primary aim of the operation was to bomb the base, but the Admiralty was anxious to get information as to the numbers and types of warships in harbour at Wilhelmshaven or anchored in the Schillig roads.

The distance was too great for seaplanes with a reasonable load of bombs operating from coastal bases in Britain, and the aircraft were therefore embarked in three seaplane carriers, the *Arethusa, Engadine,* and *Riviera,* each carrying three seaplanes. An escort of two light cruisers and eight destroyers was provided, backed up by another force of light cruisers, destroyers, and submarines. On reaching a position ten miles north of Heligoland, the seaplanes were hoisted out by cranes and lowered on to the water. Seven managed to take off, two others for some reason failed to do so and were hoisted inboard again. While awaiting the return of the raiding aircraft the naval squadron cruised around close to Heligoland. It was attacked by a German seaplane which dropped four bombs; all of them missed. A Zeppelin then appeared and the cruisers opened fire with 6-inch guns at extreme elevation with shrapnel shells, whereupon the airship withdrew. Three of the British seaplanes returned and were hoisted aboard. A second Zeppelin and several German aeroplanes approached and some bombs were dropped without scoring any hits.

When the remaining seaplanes had been away for nearly five hours it was evident that they could be no longer airborne. After a search which proved fruitless, the naval squadrons set off for home. Three of the four missing pilots were later recovered by a submarine. As soon as it had taken them aboard it was attacked by an airship, probably a Parseval, and compelled to dive. The fourth pilot, who had been forced down by engine failure, was picked up by a Dutch fishing-vessel and after a short period of detention in Holland was repatriated.

The raid was not a great success as the airship sheds were not located, but some damage was caused by bombing to German naval installations and a good deal of information gathered. It was chiefly noteworthy because it was carried out by seaplanes transported by ship to a position close to the target and then lowered on to the

Right: Bombing by hand before the incorporation of bomb racks; an airborne British naval lieutenant attacks the enemy

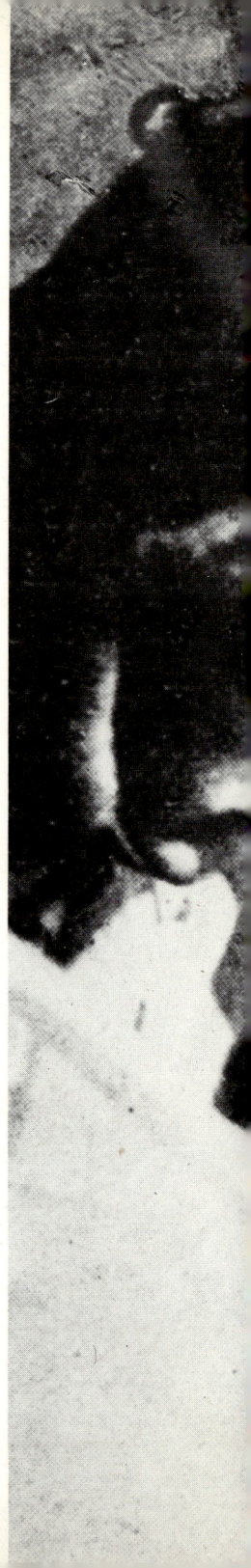

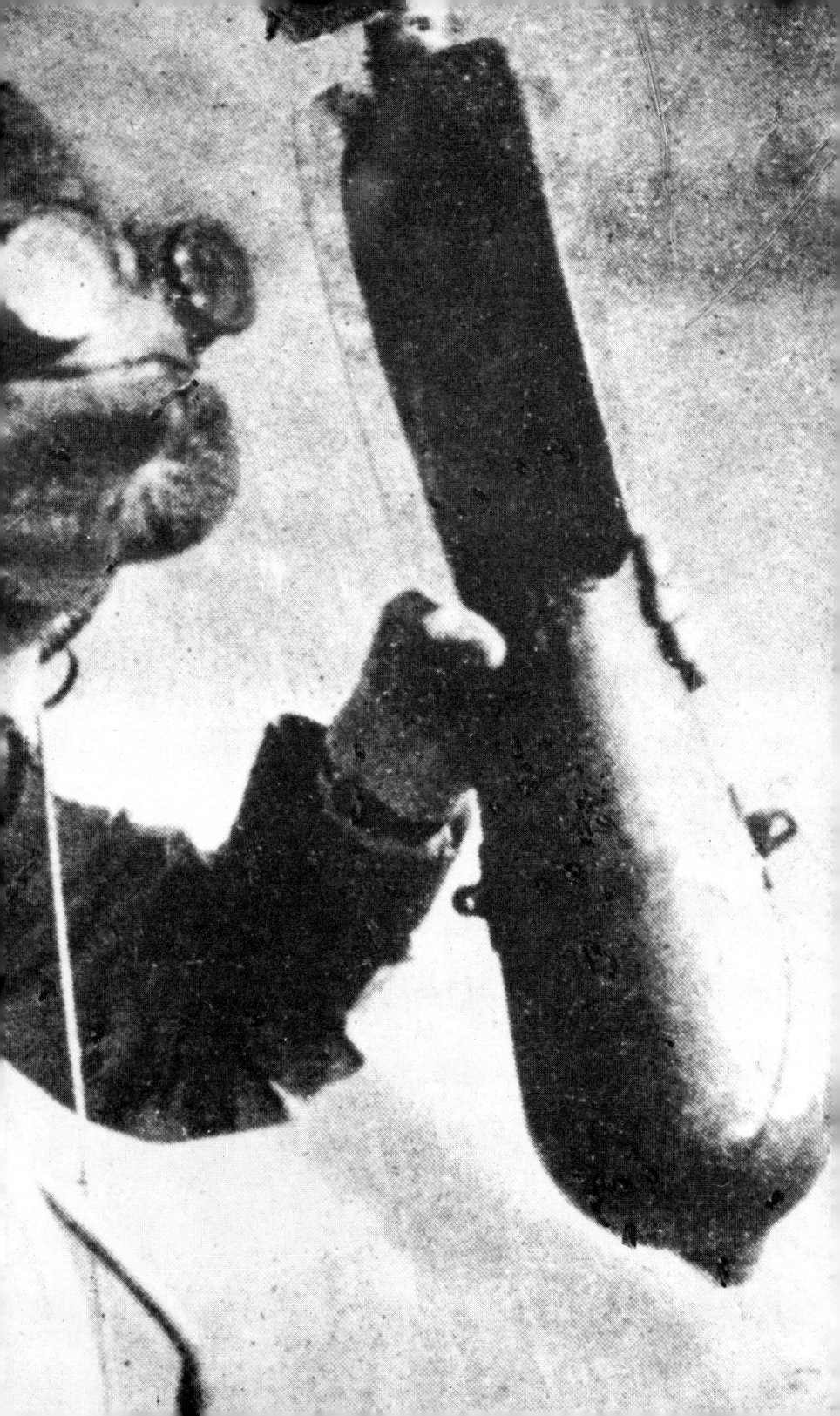

sea. And also because it brought about the first serious air/sea battle. However, it was inconclusive: the aircraft did not damage the ships, nor could the warships damage the aircraft.

On the day before the Cuxhaven raid, the Germans made their first air attack on Britain, when an aeroplane dropped one bomb harmlessly on English soil near Dover. The first Zeppelin raid occurred on the night of 19th January 1915 when two airships dropped bombs on East Anglia. Four people were killed and sixteen injured, and during the next six months several raids were carried out. But they caused few casualties and little damage.

These attacks showed that the defences were quite ineffective; few British pilots had flown at night and casualties among them were heavy. No practical system of night interception existed. A pilot had little chance of finding a Zeppelin and not much more hope of finding his own landing ground again. The complete failure of the British air defences was soon obvious to the general public. Artillery was no more successful and it was clear that the Zeppelins must be picked up and illuminated by searchlights before any success could be expected. Admiral Sir Percy Scott, an extroverted and capable naval gunnery expert, was put in charge, and the public was somewhat reassured. He had no experience, however, of dealing with targets travelling at 60 mph or more a mile or two up in the air, and the task was beyond him. It is noteworthy that, while a fair number of Zeppelins were destroyed by aeroplanes in the air and on the ground, none was ever brought down over England by anti-aircraft fire.

The menace of the Zeppelin

Bad weather, poor visibility, and strong winds caused many Zeppelin sorties against Britain to fail, and the British were even unaware that some attempts had been made. The attacks carried out so far had met with scant success but the German public, deceived by optimistic propaganda, believed that great things had been achieved. Captain Strasser and the German navy, however, knew that this was not so, and they cast about for new ideas to improve their effectiveness. Herr Hagen, a Cologne engineer, had the idea of lowering an observation capsule on a steel cable which was connected by telephone to the control gondola of the airship so that an observer could guide a ship which remained concealed in the clouds above. A prototype was fitted to an army Zeppelin L12, whose commanding officer, Captain Ernst Lehmann, had himself tested the apparatus, being lowered on a hand-winch on 600 feet of cable. He was greatly impressed by its possibilities and had a powered winch installed carrying 2,700 feet of cable incorporating an insulated tele-

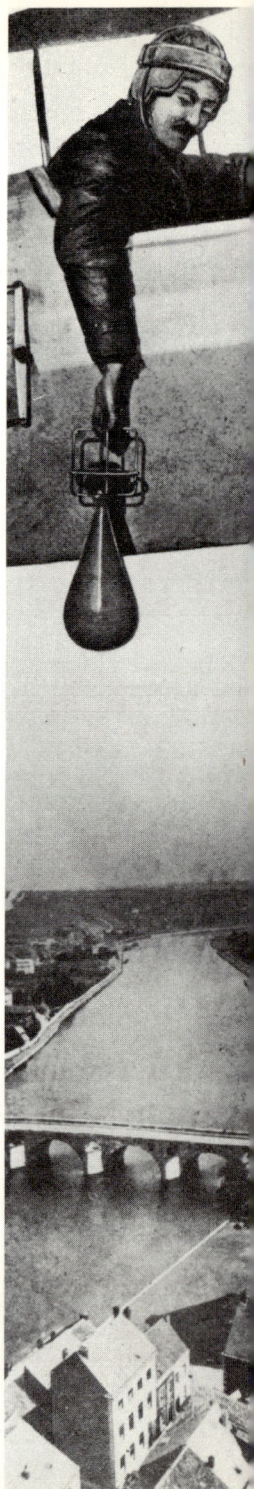

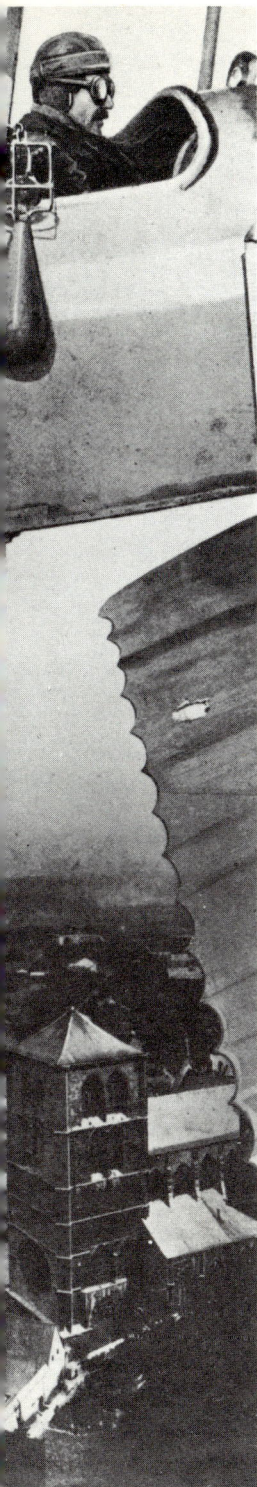

phone wire. This device was first employed during a raid on the British east coast on 17th March 1915. The weather was very bad and England was shrouded in thick low cloud, so Lehmann turned southwards hoping to see the Thames estuary. He saw nothing, so Sub-Lieutenant Max von Gemmingen, a nephew of Count Zeppelin, was lowered 2,500 feet into clear air. He found himself over Calais while the airship remained unseen in the clouds above though its engines could be heard. This apparatus was later extensively used and proved most valuable.

The German plan to bomb Britain went ahead. There is little doubt that they believed that the spirit of the British people could by this means be eroded and perhaps destroyed. The shorter-ranged army Zeppelins, using bases in Belgium, could attack London and targets in the Thames estuary, while the longer-ranged naval ships, operating from more distant bases, could attack a wider range of targets. The British defences were, however, improving, as guns and searchlights were installed in the most probable target areas and training in night-flying progressed. As yet, though several Zeppelins had been destroyed at their bases and some by accident, none had been brought down by the British air defences. Not until 7th June 1915 was one destroyed by an aeroplane.

From the autumn of 1915 to the autumn of 1916 a fair number of airship raids were made on London and south-east England. By this time it was becoming common for three or four airships to be sent on a raid. No great damage was done but public indignation was very great, especially as the defences seemed powerless to deal with the menace. These feelings subsided when, in September 1916, Captain Leefe Robinson of the RFC, using a new type of incendiary bullet called the Buckingham which was to prove a most effective weapon against airships, shot down Schutte-Lanz SL11 on the northern outskirts of London. The spectacular fall of the flaming airship was seen by a vast number of people who realised that at last the British air defences had scored a triumph.

This incident ended a long period during which German airships had cruised about over England with impunity. They did not, in fact, cause many casualties or much damage, mainly because they seldom knew where they were and could not locate worthwhile targets. Once they had found their objectives, however, their problem was relatively simple since – unlike an aeroplane – they could stop and hover over the target and drop their bombs almost vertically. During the next nine months several Zeppelins were shot down by aeroplanes of the British home defence system. The last airship to fall on British

Left: 1914 – a German bomber crew depicted over Huy, Belgium

soil was the LZ48, brought down during the night of 16th June 1917 in a joint attack by a DH2 from the Experimental Station at Orfordness and a BE12 from 39 Squadron of the Home Defences.

After this the Germans changed over to aeroplane raids on Britain, and on 7th July 1917 a daring daylight raid on London by a large formation of Gotha twin-engined bombers occurred. The defending fighters failed to intercept and the AA guns failed to score a hit. Public indignation boiled over. However, gradually air defences improved and the attacks were mainly carried out at night. Eventually these too dwindled and died away.

It is rather ironical that the British people should have been the first to suffer from air bombardment because their island home and their successful reliance on sea power for centuries had insulated them from the direct effects of military conflict. All their wars, apart from a few civil wars long ago, had been fought on the high seas or in other people's countries. This had encouraged the idea that war was the armed forces' business in which the civilian population ought not to be involved. The conquest of the air changed all this.

On the Western Front the air forces had been too preoccupied with army cooperation duties to think much about bombing. It was not until January 1915 that the RFC made its first bombing raid with an attack on the Lille railway station and the Zeppelin sheds at Ghistelle. No further attacks were made until March, just before the battle of Neuve-Chapelle. A few more attacks were then made and in the summer of 1915 RFC Headquarters reviewed the results of bombing to date. Out of 141 attacks, mainly on railway objectives by one or two aircraft, only three had been successful. As a result of this review General Trenchard prevailed upon GHQ to lay down that 'aeroplanes will not be used by armies in attempts to influence local situations by bombing railway stations and junctions. Sustained attacks with a view to interrupting the enemy's railway communications will be ordered by GHQ in conjunction with the main operations of the Allied armies. Special squadrons are being trained for this purpose.' This appears to be the first allusion to the principle of concentration in bombing, and the first attempt by GHQ to centralise the control of bombers and prevent their misuse by armies and corps. The attempt was not successful, and for the next three years British battlefield bombing was ineffective owing to lack of concentration. Too few aircraft were given too many targets.

The French did little tactical bombing, sometimes

Top left: *Italians bomb Austrian supply route.* **Bottom:** *Blitz 1915-style — a Shoreditch street after a Zeppelin airship raid*

dropping a few bombs from Caudron aircraft engaged in reconnaissance. In general they followed the British pattern and their results were no better. The Germans also rarely practised tactical bombing, but when they did they usually attacked airfields. Because they understood the principle of concentration their attacks, though rare, were usually successful.

No bomber aircraft as such had yet been produced, except the German Gotha which was intended to replace the Zeppelin for the purpose of attacking targets in England. It was a well designed twin-engined aircraft with a good range and bomb load. The British too eventually began to give serious attention to bombers and the DH9, DH4, Handley-Page 0/400, and the Vickers Vimy appeared. The DH9 was a two-seater powered by a 230 hp Beardmore engine, but this was soon replaced by the DH4, the same aeroplane with the more powerful 375 hp Rolls-Royce Eagle engine. The Handley-Page 0/400 was a large, heavy aircraft with two Rolls-Royce Eagles, capable of carrying about 2,000 lbs of bombs with a fairly long range. It was, however, too vulnerable for daylight operations and was used for night work, mainly by the RNAS. The Vickers Vimy was a smaller faster twin, powered by two Eagle engines, with a long range and good bomb load. It arrived too late in the war for much use to be made of it. Another rather late arrival was the DH9a, a much improved version of the DH9, driven by the remarkably successful Liberty engine of 400 hp. This engine was the main American contribution to the air war, and the DH9a proved to be a most useful aircraft with a long post-war career. In the autumn of 1918 the huge Handley-Page V/1500 with four Rolls-Royce Eagles appeared, but too late to play any active part in the war. It had been intended to use it to attack Berlin by night from a base in Norfolk.

Neither the French nor the Italians designed any specialised bomber aircraft; the small amount of tactical bombing that they undertook was carried out by army cooperation types.

It has always been difficult for even friends and allies to learn anything about Russian military equipment. It is certain that they entered the war with little in the way of effective aviation, although Igor Sikorski began building aeroplanes as early as 1908. An exceptionally talented designer, he built and attempted to fly a helicopter in 1909 and in 1913 he designed and built the world's first multi-engined bomber. The Russian army authorities showed little interest at first, but by 1917

Left: 1918—precursor of the V1 bomb: an early explosives-carrying, pilotless aircraft, built for the US government in Ohio

Russia was building 1,000 aeroplanes a year. This was, however, a relatively small output. One good designer does not make an air force and they had to buy Italian Ansaldos and French Caudrons, Nieuports, and Spads. The revolution in 1917, followed by the Russian military collapse and the Peace of Brest-Litovsk, put an end to the development of military aviation. Sikorski left Russia, went to France for a while, and then to America where he continued to design aircraft.

The Middle Eastern fronts followed much the same pattern as the Western, but being secondary theatres they were less well supplied with aircraft. Indeed, they proved to be, for all the nations taking part in the war except Turkey, a useful way of employing aircraft super-annuated from the West. There was, however, one remarkable exception to the relatively minor role generally played by aircraft in this theatre. After the Battle of Megiddo in September 1918 the Turkish army was forced to withdraw, using roads through hilly districts that in places were defiles. Here they were caught by Allied aircraft and everything that could fly was pressed into service. Machine-gunning by fighters and light bombing by every aircraft that could carry a bomb turned a retreat into a rout and a rout into a massacre. This was the first time that aircraft had been able to attack troops under really advantageous conditions. The result was a classical example of a successful 'pursuit', hitherto the prerogative of the cavalry. The news of this terrible slaughter caused armies everywhere to realise the tremendous offensive power of aircraft given the right conditions.

By 1917 various types of simple bomb-sights had been developed which made it possible to bomb with a fair degree of accuracy from considerable heights. And towards the end of the war two further important developments occurred. Warships had been modified to carry fighter aircraft, mainly for their own defence. It was not difficult for them to take off from a short platform but no ship could provide a level surface long enough for them to land on again. They therefore had to fly after completing their task to the nearest friendly airfield or ditch in the sea and hope for the best. This was clearly unsatisfactory and in 1918 the British battle-cruiser *Furious* was converted to an aircraft carrier. She had a long flat upper deck, almost as long as the ship, on which aircraft could land successfully. Secondly, the RNAS had modified a torpedo which could be carried and launched by an aircraft. The Turkish battleship *Mejidieh* was sunk by an airborne torpedo. The Admiralty was not pleased to hear of this, for it was unwilling to admit that aircraft could sink a warship.

On 1st April 1918 the British amalgamated the RFC

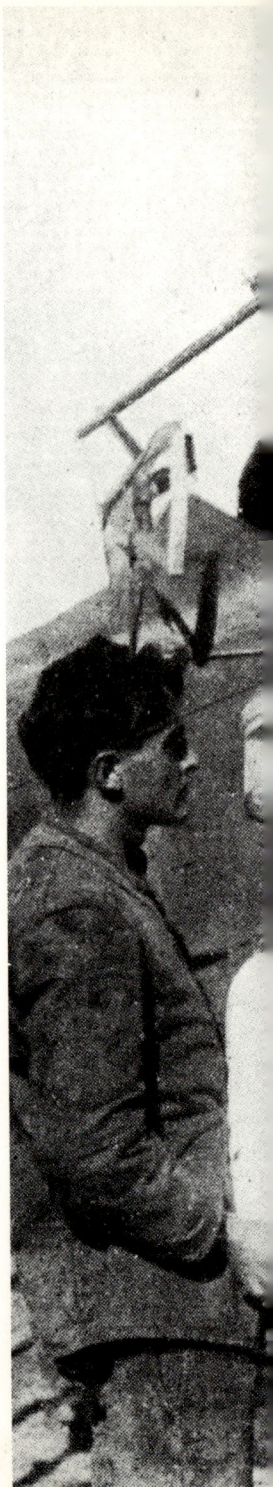

and RNAS to form the Royal Air Force, an event that was to have a very important influence on the organisation of the military aviation of all the leading powers. By the summer of 1917 the British government had become gravely dissatisfied with the organisation of its air services. The RFC was still overstretched and was unable to meet all the demands made upon it, while the RNAS, with a low casualty rate, had expanded to the point at which many of its squadrons were virtually unemployed. It was also clear that home air defence had been greatly handicapped by its division between two authorities – the Royal Navy being responsible for all activities beyond the high-water mark, and the Army for all inland defences. And it should be realised that even at this time the Admiralty and War Office had almost no experience of cooperating with each other. In the autumn of 1917 the government asked General Jan Smuts of South Africa, who was both able and impartial, to investigate the whole matter. He recommended unification with the object of making better use of the available resources and this was accepted by the government.

By the time the Royal Air Force came into being the war was within seven months of its end, and its effect was felt mainly in two directions. The squadrons of the RNAS were given full employment, relieving the RFC of some of the strain that it had borne for so long, and a new formation, the Independent Air Force (IAF), was created. The object of this was to set up a bomber force, acting independently of the British GHQ, to attack German centres of war industry and communications in the Ruhr and Rhineland. It never possessed more than eleven squadrons of DH9's and DH4's, capable of carrying 500 lbs of bombs to a radius of action of about 100 miles. In order to emphasise its independence, it was situated behind the French army front and controlled directly by the newly formed Air Ministry. Some of its attacks were successful, far more successful than previous bombing raids by any country, but it cannot be said that it achieved decisive – or even very positive – results. It certainly annoyed the German government, had some adverse effect on war production and civilian morale, and drew off a number of fighter squadrons from the Western Front to strengthen the German air defences.

Had the war not ended when it did it is interesting to speculate on what might have happened if the four-engined Handley-Pages had attacked Berlin. It seems likely that once again weather and engine trouble would have been more formidable than the enemy fighters or AA defences.

Left: Packing the punch – an Italian plane is loaded with bombs

Chapter 6
Reorganisation and Controversy

When the war ended in an Allied victory the intensive development of aviation that had taken place in all the belligerent nations, except Russia and Turkey, came to an abrupt end. In the defeated nations military aviation was forbidden by the peace treaties, and among the victors the cry was for retrenchment and a return to peace-time conditions. Before the war there had been no commercial aviation and so there was nothing to revive.

The vast air forces that had been so hastily created were even more rapidly demobilised. Since there were huge stocks of airframes, engines, bombs, machine-guns, and ammunition, and large numbers of trained pilots and observers, a period of stagnation set in. Factories stood idle or were converted to other uses and the training schools were almost empty or closed down. All over the world there was a pause for reflection and reorganisation.

There was a strong tendency to revert to pre-war conditions in the fighting forces. Cavalry took priority over tanks, and bands and ceremonial drill over aircraft. Military aviation had gravely complicated the art of war and its senior practitioners, with few exceptions, were anxious to see it suppressed or at least brought under firm control. In France alone was a reasonable-sized air service kept in being, estimated in 1920 at about 1,000 first-line aircraft. In Russia everything was still in hopeless turmoil after the Bolshevik Revolution and the fighting that followed it, and the need to combat mass starvation precluded any attempt to rebuild their moribund aviation. In Italy the Regia Aeronautica maintained its existence but at a low level of activity. America, relieved at the satisfactory ending of the war, sank back into isolation and her armed forces — apart from the navy — were reduced almost to vanishing point. In Britain the newly-formed Royal Air Force was under powerful attack from the two older services. They fully believed that it was a war-time expedient, like conscription or the Ministry of Munitions, and that the coming of peace would

Left: Father of the RAF — Lord Trenchard (shading his eyes), photographed shortly before the start of the Second World War

see its abolition and the restoration of subordinate army and naval air services. They contended with some truth that the war had ended without providing any positive proof of the offensive power of aircraft. The Admiralty refused to admit that aircraft could sink or even seriously damage any warship under operational conditions, or that they were ever likely to be able to do so. Both the older services insisted that aircraft were of value only in direct support of land or sea operations.

Trenchard, the Chief of the Air Staff, had very different ideas and was determined to maintain the RAF as a separate third service. He had no great practical experience as an airman and was no abstract theorist, but he had an inspired prophetic vision of quite remarkable accuracy. The way in which he regularly defeated men apparently cleverer and more articulate than himself was a perpetual source of amazement to his staff.

His strongest argument was that the flexibility, power of concentration, and offensive capacity of an air force— which were its greatest assets—would be largely destroyed if it were divided and placed under the control of the Army and navy. He pointed out that it was precisely this fatal weakness which in the stark reality of war had made it necessary to form the RAF. Only by maintaining a unified service could the most effective and economical use be made of the available resources in aircraft and manpower. Since economy was, as always, the main preoccupation of the British government in defence matters this argument carried much weight, but its advantages were more apparent in war than in peace. The weakness of Trenchard's position—especially in an era following what had been called 'the war to end war'—was that the RAF was superimposed on the older pattern of imperial defence. Its existence did not permit compensating reductions in the strength of the Army or the navy.

Most other countries had ended the war with separate military and naval air services, and they watched Britain with very great interest to see what was going to happen. None did so with greater attention than the United States where there had been growing dissatisfaction within their own organisation. The American airmen realised that the army and the navy were determined to reduce and keep under firm control what they regarded as their restive and precocious air units.

Civilian populations everywhere had heard about the air bombardments of Britain and the Rhineland and were deeply apprehensive about the possible threat to their status as non-combatants. Their fears were not allayed by the pronouncements of those who expounded the

Right: 1923—instructors at Cranwell, the RAF's Sandhurst

theories of air power. Prominent among these was an Italian, General Giulio Douhet, a man of advanced ideas. In 1921 he wrote a book called *The Command of the Air* in which he insisted that the air force must be an independent service, under the control of neither the army nor the navy. He believed that war had become total; the entire resources and population of a nation would be bound to be sucked into 'the maw of war'. He insisted that aircraft could 'go far behind the fortified lines of defence without first breaking through them'. He emphasised the unity and the all-pervading character of the air ocean, and its freedom from all barriers and obstacles. Douhet stressed the importance of gaining command of the air from the very beginning of a war. 'All the influences,' he wrote, 'which have conditioned and characterised warfare from the beginning are powerless to affect aerial action. No longer can areas exist in which life can be lived in safety and tranquillity, nor can the battlefield be limited to actual combatants.' All citizens of a country at war would, he claimed, 'become combatants, since all will be exposed to the aerial offensives of the enemy. There will be no distinction any longer between soldiers and civilians.' He went on to assert that the classical doctrine which held that the principal aim in war must be the destruction of the enemy armed forces, though still valid for armies and navies operating in two dimensions, no longer governed the activities of air forces. He emphasised the powerful moral and material effects of heavy air attacks on capital cities and other centres of administration, communications, and production. It is of particular interest to note his insistence on the importance of concentration, since neglect of this principle had led during the war to a vast amount of wasted effort. It was, indeed, the main reason for the relative ineffectiveness of much aerial bombing.

Douhet recalled that during the First World War neither side had been able to deliver against the other a really heavy blow, concentrated in time and space. It is true that the casualties added up at the end to an appalling total, but they had resembled the Chinese 'death of a thousand cuts'. It had been a war of attrition, which Douhet thought was the cruellest way to wage war. He believed that half the damage and casualties would have sufficed to gain victory for either side if they could have been inflicted in three months instead of four years, and a quarter would have sufficed if it had been inflicted in eight days. Air forces, he believed, were ideally suited to concentrated attacks against an enemy's vital centres, and that by such means it was possible to paralyse the enemy's power of waging war.

This book caused grave offence in almost all quarters.

It was severely criticised by most soldiers and sailors and condemned by civilians throughout the world. Douhet suffered the fate of most prophets: he was savagely attacked in his own country and elsewhere. Scorn and ridicule were poured upon his book, and even some airmen believed that he had gone too far. It is worthy of note that his writings were not recommended reading at the RAF Staff College. No doubt he was ahead of his time. But all that has happened since has amply confirmed his views.

It is not surprising that statesmen in many countries began to work for international agreements abolishing or severely limiting air bombardment, except for tactical purposes in a battle zone against strictly military targets.

The role of the RAF
Meanwhile, in Britain the RAF continued its precarious existence. Trenchard was convinced that if the RAF could not discover a way of taking over some of the existing responsibilities of the Army or the navy, thus permitting a reduction in land or sea forces to compensate for its cost, it would continue to be vulnerable. Strategic and military considerations unfortunately cut little ice in peacetime and it seemed probable that sooner or later a British government would decide that it could no longer afford what could be represented as the luxury of a separate Air Ministry. Trenchard realised, however, that the Army and navy had no intention of allowing the RAF to take over any of their responsibilities. Indeed, they regarded the very idea as ludicrous.

A serious rebellion in Iraq in 1920 gave Trenchard the opportunity he was looking for. The British government had accepted a mandate for the new state of Iraq from the League of Nations. This meant that the mandatory power would be responsible for the internal and external security of the embryo state, and would help it economically until it was able to stand on its feet. When that position had been reached the mandatory power would sponsor the application of its protégé for membership of the League, and it was hoped that the ex-mandatory power and the new state would conclude a treaty of friendship and possibly a military alliance.

The rebellion in Iraq, which was on a serious scale, put the British forces, consisting of two-and-a-half divisions of British and Indian troops, in a position of some difficulty and even danger and caused acute embarrassment to the British government. It was suppressed after severe fighting, but it was clear that the mandate might involve Britain for a long period in serious casualties and high military expenditure. Iraq was poor and turbulent,

Left: *Iraq's King Feisal in the cockpit of an RAF Vickers Vernon*

menaced by Turkey in the north and by Saudi Arabia in the south-west. No oil had as yet been discovered in Iraq and no economic or other advantage could be discerned in Britain's association with this remote and little-known land. A strong movement developed in Britain which urged that the mandate should be handed back to the League of Nations and that the British government should cut its losses and abandon the Middle East. This the government was unwilling to do, as it knew full well that if it did so the whole area would be plunged into war. It was especially apprehensive about the fate of the small Jewish enclave in Palestine, which Britain had sponsored, and which, if she withdrew, would be liable to expulsion or even massacre at the hands of the Arabs.

The dilemma was serious and a conference was called in Cairo, under the chairmanship of Winston Churchill, to consider ways and means. After hearing the estimates for military control of the area the conference was at a loss for it realised that the cost would never be accepted by the British people. At this point Trenchard intervened with a plan for air control. He admitted that the system was untried but it had been very carefully considered by the Air Staff and he felt quite confident that it would succeed. Though clearly a bit of a gamble the conference agreed to try it, in the absence of any viable alternative, as it promised to reduce by some seventy per cent the estimated costs. Such an immense saving justified an element of risk.

The main idea of air control can be briefly summarised. Under the military system, when disorders beyond the control of the police occurred in some more or less remote area the only way of dealing with the situation was to send out a column of troops. Since this was an expensive business the decision to do so was usually deferred until the situation had become intolerable. As soon as the column left its base it was liable to meet with opposition from the inhabitants of the country through which it had to pass to reach its objective. Typically these inhabitants opposed the troops partly because they had guilty consciences over past, perhaps undiscovered misdemeanours, partly because they resented the intrusion of the troops on principle, but largely because they enjoyed a scrap and hoped for loot in the form of rifles, ammunition, and so forth. The troops, therefore, had to fight their way against people with whom they had no quarrel. When, after a painfully slow and well-advertised advance, the column eventually reached the seat of the trouble, they would find that the inhabitants had fled taking everything moveable with them. The column could do no more

Right: Sopwith Snipes of the RAF on patrol over Baghdad, 1926

than burn or destroy the houses, the only things that the offenders could not take with them. The column could not stay long, and on the return journey they would again have to fight every yard of the way and any miscalculation of food or ammunition supplies could, and sometimes did, cause disaster. The history of the north-west frontier of India contains many examples of such terrible failures.

Under the system of air control, when the police or local political officers reported unrest or disorder action could be taken immediately at minimal cost and risk. The offenders would be ordered to submit themselves for trial in a court of law. If they refused or committed further crimes they would be warned that on a certain date their village would be bombed. They would be told to leave the village and warned that it would not be safe for them to return until the offenders had submitted themselves to the due process of law. The bombing was light as it was not necessary, nor indeed desirable, to cause serious damage. Delayed action fuses could be used to reinforce the periodical bombing.

Properly conducted, the method of air control never failed. Sooner or later the interruption of the rebels' daily life became intolerable and with no hope of ending their predicament the most intransigent law-breakers would have to surrender. They would then go for trial and a body of police or troops would be flown in with medical staff and supplies to quell looting, treat wounds, cure disease, distribute food, and generally restore normal conditions. Damage and casualties on both sides were negligible, and were confined to those involved in the troubles.

By finding a task within the framework of the British defence system which substituted air forces for land forces and did the job far more cheaply, humanely, and efficiently, Trenchard was able to maintain the existence of the RAF against a long series of attacks from many quarters. Airmen everywhere were showing increasing dissatisfaction at their division and subordination to armies and navies, whose chiefs seemed to them to have little or no understanding of the potentialities of aircraft.

Air power controversies in the United States
In America the Naval Air Service did not chafe unduly at its subordination to the navy, but the Army Air Corps took a very different view. Its leaders were thinking along lines that were anathema to the War Department. The success of the RAF encouraged them to demand a unified air force. They had a strong faith in the importance of strategic air bombardment and there was an insistent demand for a long-range heavy bomber. The army authorities were determined to suppress these ideas, and

this caused resentment among the able and enthusiastic younger leaders of the Air Corps. Prominent among these was Brigadier-General William Mitchell, Assistant Chief of the Army Air Corps from 1919 to 1925. He was a distinguished airman who combined ability and experience with an unusually forceful personality. Realising the traditional importance of sea-power in the US defence organisation, Billy Mitchell concentrated his attacks mainly against the navy. He claimed that aeroplanes could sink any warship by means of bombs and torpedoes, but his repeated requests for target ships, in order to test his theories, were ignored. In 1920 the navy decided to mount some very inadequate trials under its own conditions, but increasing pressure from Congress compelled it to abandon this idea. In 1921 three former German warships—the battleship *Ostfriesland,* the cruiser *Frankfurt,* and a destroyer—were made available for bombing trials in Chesapeake Bay. With a hurriedly assembled bomber force Mitchell sank all three ships. The navy was furious and much argument raged about the validity of these trials. But no one could deny the fact of the sinkings. Encouraged, Mitchell went on to sink the old US battleships *Alabama* later in 1921, and *Virginia* and *New Jersey* in 1923.

These experiments aroused a tremendous amount of interest throughout the world and especially in Britain. Mitchell made full use of them to further his demand for a separate air service and this made the army and navy chiefs determined to clip his wings. He was removed from his post and banished to the Eighth Corps (Army) Area at San Antonio. Mitchell was too ardent to bear this exile with patience and he published a statement in the press on the occasion of the loss of the naval airship *Shenandoah* accusing the army and navy of neglecting—and even sabotaging—military aviation. He was recalled to Washington and tried by general court martial on charges of insubordination. Found guilty, he was suspended from duty for five years, and soon afterwards resigned his commission.

Mitchell's service career was over, but his ideas continued to find expression in his writings. In 1921 he had written a book called *Our Air Force: The Keystone of National Defence,* followed in 1925 by one called *Winged Defence,* in which he claimed that air power had brought with it new doctrines of war and that the basis of air power was the bomber aircraft. His martyrdom in the cause of air power gave force to his views—which closely resembled those of Trenchard—although it was to be many years before they were translated into action.

Left: Bomber tests, 1921—Mitchell's pilots attack a target

The American people had to wait until the disaster at Pearl Harbor to see his ideas fully vindicated.

Thus we can see that while the end of the war had brought stagnation to the material development of aircraft and engines, it also brought an effervescent activity of thought about the ways in which air power – a new concept – ought to be organised and employed.

The air forces in peacetime

But in terms of strength, all air forces continued to suffer a decline. Soon after the end of the war the British government, influenced by a public which had not forgotten the air raids, had undertaken that the RAF would possess a first-line strength not less than that of any air force within striking distance. A committee under Lord Salisbury had in 1923 recommended the creation of a substantial home defence air force, but no action had been taken. At home the RAF had been allowed to fall to a very low level. There were only four flying-boat squadrons for coastal patrol and five army cooperation squadrons in Britain. There was not a single fighter or bomber squadron at home at that time. Overseas there were two fighter squadrons and some fifteen squadrons equipped with light bomber or army cooperation types.

As for other European powers: in France the air forces, though greatly reduced, had not been so severely cut down as in Britain or Italy. German military aviation had been banned by the Treaty of Versailles and the war-shattered Turks had nothing to speak of. Soviet Russia was recovering slowly, very slowly, from the effects of the Revolution and Civil War, and though it appeared probable that she would have an air force in time, there was as yet little sign of it. However, in the early 1920s A.N. Tupelov, later to become a world-famous designer, and Professor N.E. Zhukovski began seriously to study aircraft engineering. By 1922 the Soviet government realised that it had fallen far behind the rest of the world in the development of aviation and that the very vastness of Russia underlined the importance of air transport. As an interim measure the Russians bought aircraft from France, Italy, Holland, and Britain. It was, however, the Treaty of Versailles, which denied military air forces to the Germans, that did most to help the progress of Russian aeronautics. Thousands of young Germans whose enthusiasm for aviation had been stimulated by the war turned to Russia for an outlet for this interest. In 1921-2 secret agreements were signed between Germany and the USSR for technical aid to the Russian aircraft industry, and the Germans gained facilities for flying training.

Right: Champion of strategic air power – General William Mitchell

German airmen served in Russian military units and thus kept alive a cadre of well-trained and practical airmen in defiance of the Treaty of Versailles. This cooperation was valuable to the Russians but even more so to the Germans. In 1922 several hundred Soviet officers were given a course in advanced military studies in Berlin and in return the German firm of Junkers was permitted to establish an aircraft factory near Moscow.

In these circumstances — since the Russo-German agreement was secret — it was impossible to discern a threat to the security of any country through air action. With regard to the pledge by the British government, the Italians, Russians, and Americans were out of range, and it was impossible to imagine that the French air force was likely to attack Britain. Nor did any country in Europe fear a British air attack. Thus the period was one in which all countries felt reasonably secure. It is, therefore, understandable that few advances in military aviation were made, though there were some practical innovations. Parachutes for aircrews were introduced, bomb and gun sights were improved, and systematic training in night-flying was begun.

Right: US airship Shenandoah, *destroyed in a storm in 1923*

Chapter 7
The Dawn of Commercial Aviation

The lack of progress in military aviation during the post-war years was balanced by an awakening interest in aircraft as a means of rapid communication, and stagnation in the military sphere encouraged air enthusiasts to turn their attention to the problem of air transport. There had been a few civilian long-distance flights before the war, beginning with the famous race in 1910 from London to Manchester for the prize of £10,000 offered by the *Daily Mail*. This aroused tremendous public interest, although there were only two serious competitors – Louis Paulhan in a Farman and Claude Grahame-White in an aeroplane of his own design called the 'box-kite'. Paulhan won in a flying-time of 4 hours 12 minutes over the 183 miles, though the journey was not completed in one day. This was not very promising as the rail journey in those days by the splendid service of the old London & North Western Railway took only a little over three hours. But aircraft were still slow, had no great range, and their engines were notoriously unreliable.

In America William Randolph Hearst, a wealthy newspaper owner, offered in 1911 a prize of 50,000 dollars for a flight across America between the Atlantic and Pacific coasts. Calbraith P. Rodgers, a free-lance pilot flying a Wright biplane, completed the journey in slow time in a series of short hops involving nineteen more or less serious crashes. But he arrived too late to qualify for the prize. In November of the same year Ruth Law Oliver, a famous American woman pilot, flew from Chicago to New York, a distance of 512 miles, in the remarkable time of 5 hours 40 minutes. No doubt she was helped by a strong tail-wind, but it was an impressive performance.

Civil aviation, like its military counterpart, did not lack its prophets and enthusiasts, but they had been frustrated during the war by the overwhelming concentration on military aviation. Now they saw some hope of their dreams coming true. But the problems were formidable. Airfields were very few and far between;

Left: Commercial enterprise and the pioneer spirit – two vital ingredients in the rapid post-war development of aviation

107

THE NEW YORK HERALD.

NEW YORK, MONDAY, JUNE 16, 1919.   PRICE TWO CENTS

TWO BRITISH FLYERS MAKE 1,900 MILE DASH ACROSS ATLANTIC TO IRELAND IN 16 HOURS; ALCOCK AND BROWN WIN $50,000 PRIZE

THE VICKERS VIMY AIRPLANE

2,000 WORD SUMMARY OF GERMAN COUNTER PROPOSALS MADE PUBLIC; FOE TO GET NEW TREATY TODAY

GERMANY IS ALLOWED ARMY OF 200,000 MEN

Air Routes Across Atlantic

VICKERS-VIMY BIPLANE LANDS AT CLIFDEN AFTER A PERFECT FLIGHT AT 120 MILES AN HOUR

KING SENDS HIS CONGRATULATIONS TO PILOT

AMERICAN TROOPS CROSS RIO GRANDE AND ENTER JUAREZ

Twenty-Fourth Infantry, with 1,000 Men, Now on Mexican Soil.

TO PREVENT DAMAGE ON AMERICAN SIDE

Congress to Take Action This Week in Regard to Muzzling of Dr. Ellis

Representative Mott Has Resolution Directing State Department to Investigate Charges That British and American Officials in Egypt Are Hampering Herald Correspondent.

GERMANS WILL GET

KING GEORGE SENDS WARMEST CONGRATULATIONS TO AIRMEN

air navigation was usually by dead-reckoning, though some astro-navigation of a rough and ready kind had been attempted. Fog, icing-up, and storms caused serious hazards. In addition, every nation was deemed to own the air above its territory *usque ad coelum* (to the sky) and passing through it without express permission for each flight was regarded as a serious violation of national sovereignty.

In February 1919 a Department of Civil Aviation was established within the British Air Ministry to authorise and control civil flying. Regulations for air navigation were being drawn up by many countries, and in a number of instances reciprocal over-flying rights were negotiated. These applied only to commercial aviation, and permission for the passage of military aircraft had to be specially arranged and planned for each flight and the prescribed routes strictly adhered to. Some countries declared prohibited zones from which all aircraft, civil and military, were barred.

The year 1919 was notable for the pioneering of long-distance flights. In March a regular air mail service, operated by the RAF, was begun between Folkestone and Cologne for the benefit of the British Army of Occupation in Germany. In May the first crossing of the Atlantic Ocean by air was achieved by an American flying-boat, the NC4, powered by four 400 hp Liberty engines. It was an epic journey. Four of these fine boats had been constructed, with reinforced hulls designed to stand up to heavy seas. It was intended to fly all four aircraft across the Atlantic to Britain. NC2 was, however, destroyed in a fire in a hangar at Far Rockaway, New York, and thus only the three remaining boats set off. NC1 and NC3 reached Trepassey Bay in Newfoundland without incident after a flight of over 1,000 miles. NC4 encountered trouble and one engine had to be switched off. Not long afterwards another engine broke a connecting-rod and the aircraft was forced down off Cape Cod, Massachusetts, finally succeeding in taxi-ing to the Naval Air Station at Chatham. The wrecked engine was replaced, and the NC4 reached Trepassey Bay after an overnight stop at Halifax, Nova Scotia.

Further engine trouble required more engine replacements, but at last all three boats were ready to attempt the next stage of the flight to the Azores. They took off, each aircraft flying separately. The weather, in spite of favourable forecasts, turned very bad with much cloud and sea fog. NC3 lost its way and came down on the sea.

Top, left: June 1919—Alcock and Brown are headline news.
Bottom: Alan Cobham cheered after his flight from Australia, 1926. Top, right: NC4 arrives in Lisbon from North America

After riding out very rough weather for 52 hours, during which the aircraft was damaged, it finally reached the island of Ponta Delgada in the eastern Azores by taxi-ing under its own power. The aircraft needed very extensive repairs and could go no further. The fact that it had not sunk, however, was a tribute to its sound design and construction. NC1 also got lost, and came down on the sea about 100 miles west of the island of Flores in the western Azores. It was spotted by the SS *Ionia* and the crew were rescued, but an attempt to tow the battered aircraft through heavy seas failed and it soon disintegrated and sank. NC4, hitherto the unlucky one, fared better and arrived safely at Horta, going on next day to Ponta Delgada. After a week spent in servicing the aircraft and resting the crew, NC4 left for Lisbon where it arrived after a flight of $9\frac{1}{2}$ hours, thus becoming the first aircraft to cross the Atlantic. Three days later it flew on to Plymouth, receiving a great welcome from the crowd at the waterfront. The flight had taken fifteen days.

In April 1919 an unsuccessful attempt to fly non-stop from Newfoundland to Ireland was made by a well-known test pilot, Harry Hawker, with Lieutenant-Commander Mackenzie-Grieve as navigator, in a specially built Sopwith biplane. The two airmen were forced to come down in mid-Atlantic with engine trouble near the Danish vessel SS *Mary*. They were rescued, but since the ship had no radio were given up as lost. They were eventually landed at Scapa Flow in the Orkneys, and were welcomed home amid scenes of great excitement and relief.

At last, in June 1919, the first non-stop crossing of the Atlantic by air was achieved. On 14th June John Alcock and Arthur Whitten-Brown left Newfoundland in a modified Vickers Vimy fitted with extra petrol tanks. The take-off was tricky as the aircraft was seriously overloaded, but Alcock was a very able and experienced pilot. The radio failed soon after take-off owing to the shearing off of the small airscrew driving the electric generator. The weather was not as good as had been forecast — no uncommon thing over the Atlantic. They had no blind-flying instruments — none were then available — and they had much difficulty in flying through great masses of turbulent storm clouds, lightning, and lashing rain. At length, to their great relief, they saw land below them through a break in the clouds and decided to land. Unfortunately, what they took to be a grass field proved to be a bog, and the Vimy's wheels sank into the soft ground, breaking both undercarriages and tipping the aircraft on to its nose. It was seriously damaged, but luckily both airmen were unhurt — and they had managed to reach

Left: 1926 — civilised comfort on the London-Paris air route

1909
Calais to Dover
Louis Blériot (French)

1910
London to Manchester
Louis Paulhan (French)

1919
St John's Newfoundland to Ireland
Alcock and Brown (UK)

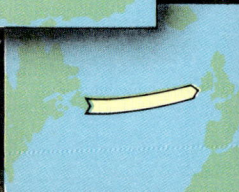

1919
Britain to Australia
Ross and Keith Smith (UK)

1922
San Diego to Indianapolis
Kelly and Macready (USA)

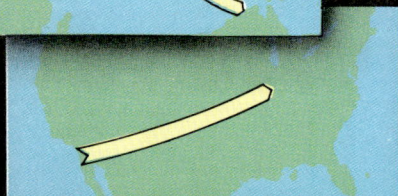

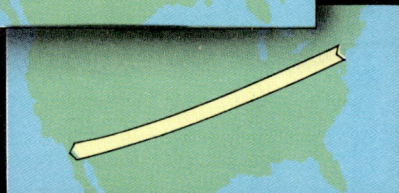

1923
New York City to San Diego
Kelly and Macready (USA)

1924 **London to Rangoon**
Alan Cobham (UK)

1924 **Circumnavigation of globe**
(Seattle-Japan-India-Europe-Iceland-Greenland-Seattle) by a team of US fliers

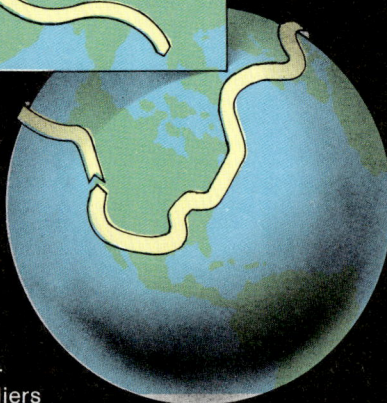

Ireland. The flight had taken 16 hours 12 minutes, and the distance was just short of 1,700 miles. They received a tumultuous welcome and gained a *Daily Mail* prize of £10,000.

These successes stimulated the competitive instincts of the lighter-than-air enthusiasts, and plans were made for a double crossing of the Atlantic by the British rigid airship R34. The design of this ship followed very closely that of the German Zeppelins. Under the command of Major G.H. Scott, with a crew of thirty, it left the RAF airship base at East Fortune in Scotland on 2nd July. A member of the crew who was left out at the last moment, an air mechanic named Ballantyne, achieved notoriety by stowing away in the airship. (He was not discovered until the ship was well on its way, but he was leniently dealt with and later became a sergeant-pilot.) R34 arrived at Mineola, New York, after a flight of 3,260 miles lasting four days and seven hours. Interestingly, the airship had not been able to improve much on the time of the fastest Atlantic liners. After three days the R34 left on its homeward journey, arriving on 9th July. Although considerable mechanical trouble of various kinds was encountered on this 6,500 mile journey, it could mostly be dealt with in the air and had not caused a forced landing. The success of this double crossing of the vast and stormy Atlantic Ocean was everywhere greeted with great acclaim. The safety and comfort of travel by airship, in contrast to the perils and hardships of open cockpit aeroplanes, made a great impression. The lighter-than-air enthusiasts were enraptured and many people were confirmed in their belief that the airship was likely to be the long-range air transport of the future.

Nevertheless, heavier-than-air craft continued to have successes. In November 1919 occurred the famous flight from Britain to Australia in a Vickers Vimy by the remarkable brothers Ross and Keith Smith. Both had served in the RAF; Ross was a first-rate pilot and Keith an exceptionally skilled navigator. They encountered more than their fair share of bad weather and various troubles on their long flight, especially in the later stages, but their resourcefulness and determination overcame all obstacles. In order to fly such long stages non-stop they had to fit extra petrol tanks, and the take-off of so heavily laden an aircraft from indifferently constructed airfields was not the least of their trials. The flight was completed in a little under twenty-eight days, just in time to win the prize of £10,000 offered by the Australian government.

Early in 1920 Colonel Pierre van Ryneveld and Flight-Lieutenant Quintin Brand took off from England in a

Left: Blazing the air trails – epic flights from 1909 to 1924

Vimy for Cape Town. They suffered many mishaps. Such airfields as were available were mostly rough, certainly unready for their arrival, and their journey was lengthy and full of adventure. They eventually reached Cape Town, after more than six weeks, in a borrowed DH9.

The early 1920s saw a number of other important long-distance flights. In September 1922 Lieutenant James H. Doolittle (later a famous general in the Second World War) made the first coast to coast flight in America in a single day. He flew a DH4b from Pablo Beach, Florida, to San Diego, California, a distance of 2,163 miles, in just under $21\frac{1}{2}$ hours' flying time, a very remarkable effort. This was followed in May 1923 by a splendid flight of 2,520 miles from New York to San Diego, in a little less than 27 hours, by Lieutenants Kelly and Macready in a Fokker T2. Between November 1924 and March 1925 Alan Cobham made the first of his famous long-distance flights. This was from London to Rangoon and back in a DH50, carrying Sir Sefton Brancker, then British Director-General of Civil Aviation. Later in 1925 Cobham flew the same aircraft from London to Cape Town and back.

Finally between April and September 1924 the first circumnavigation of the world was accomplished by a team of American airmen flying four specially designed Douglas amphibian aircraft, capable of alighting on and taking off from land or water. Their route was Seattle-Japan-India-Europe-Iceland-Greenland-Seattle. The journey took 175 days, with a total flying-time of some 360 hours for each aircraft—an average of about 70 mph. The overall time was not impressive; after all Jules Verne had shown many years before that it was possible to go round the world in eighty days. But it was a great achievement, nevertheless, requiring first-class airmanship and sound organisation, and it sign-posted the way for later progress.

When evaluating all these flights it must be remembered that apart from difficulties caused by unreliable engines, supplies of aviation fuel and spare parts had to be sent ahead to selected airfields along the route and any failure to reach the next scheduled stop could cause very serious delays.

The triumphs of these pioneers naturally stimulated interest in the commercial possibilities of the new form of transport. Early in 1919 a German civil air company was already operating a somewhat irregular service between Berlin, Leipzig, and Weimar, and in August a rather sporadic passenger service was inaugurated between London and Paris by the Air Travel and Transport Company. At first converted DH9s were used on the London-Paris route. In these open aircraft passengers had

Right: Croydon Airport—the London area's first air terminus

114

to wear flying helmets and heavy overcoats, and they were charged £21 for a single journey. Business was not very brisk. Nevertheless, other services were opened up. In March 1920 Croydon was designated as London's terminal airport for traffic from the Continent, and in May the Royal Dutch Airline (KLM) began regular flights between Rotterdam and London. Also in 1920 a regular air service was instituted between Key West in Florida and Cuba, and in November the Queensland and Northern Territories Air Service (QANTAS) was formed. Owing to the vast distances involved and the poor alternative means of communication, the latter service filled a very important rôle and was successful from the beginning.

The carrying capacity of the converted military aeroplanes used in all these early services was so small that even with high fares the revenue from passenger travel could not cover costs. And indeed the immediate future of air transport seemed to lie in the carriage of mails rather than passengers. When an RAF officer tried to book a passage on a newly-instituted and rather amateurish French service operated by war-time Breguet bombers between Toulouse and Rabat in Morocco, the airline did its best to discourage him. The manager explained that he much preferred carrying mail rather than passengers because the former was much more profitable and less vexatious. If an accident occurred and an aircraft carrying only mail crashed in flames and was *tout carbonisé*, it was not difficult to sort things out. But if the same thing happened to passengers, it was a very different matter. 'You have no idea,' he said, 'of the extraordinary fuss and bother that is made by the relatives when something of that kind happens.'

In America, even before the end of the war, the US Post Office had started carrying air mail, at first between places where the land or sea routes were exceptionally circuitous or difficult. Later, regular services between the major cities were undertaken, but this task – without proper weather stations, with open-cockpit aircraft, and without blind-flying instruments or de-icing equipment – proved very dangerous. An especially formidable section was that between New York and Chicago over the storm-troubled Allegheny Mountains. The Post Office persisted for a time in its efforts to maintain a nation-wide airmail service, but when thirty-one out of the forty pilots under contract to carry mails had been killed, the task was handed over to private airmail companies. They were not, however, much more successful. There was a gradual improvement, but it was not until February 1921 that mail was flown from coast to coast (San Francisco-New

Left: *Early Air France passenger – cabaret star Mistinguette*

York) in just over thirty-three hours – a remarkable effort.

In June 1921 the RAF began a two-way weekly mail service between Cairo and Baghdad. The overland and sea route, via Trieste, Alexandria, Karachi, and Basrah, took twenty-eight days from London to Baghdad; the air route took from five to ten days. This was an enormous advantage to the large number of British service personnel in Iraq. The air route lay eastwards from Heliopolis airfield near Cairo, across the Suez Canal and along the coast to Gaza, and then over the northern end of the Dead Sea and the Judean mountains to Ziza, a military landing ground not far from Amman in Jordan. After refuelling, the aircraft flew 600 miles over the waterless desert to Ramadi on the Euphrates, and then to the important RAF base at Hinaidi, seven miles south of Baghdad. Since navigation across the featureless waste of the desert was difficult and the search for a lost aircraft might be lengthy, expensive, and possibly unsuccessful, a deep furrow was driven across the desert by a tractor-drawn plough as a navigation aid. This was possible because the Syrian desert, unlike the Sahara or the Empty Quarter, is not sandy but consists of firm, hard gravel and dried-up mud-flats. Suitable areas were marked as landing grounds at convenient intervals for use by aircraft in any kind of trouble. This worked extremely well; the furrow remained visible from the air for many years.

The Cairo-Baghdad air mail was the first really useful and reliable service of its kind. At first DH4s were used to carry the mail but they were soon replaced by the Vickers Vernon. This was a modification of the Vimy which had done so well in the early long-distance flights. The original bomber fuselage was replaced by a large plywood hull capable of carrying up to sixteen passengers.

By the end of the first half of the 1920s, the organisation of commercial services was taking on an advanced shape in several areas. In Britain, in April 1924, Imperial Airways was formed by the amalgamation of Handley-Page Transport, Instone Air Lines, Daimler Airways, and the British Marine Air Navigation. Daily air services between London and Paris were resumed. The company received a government subsidy but was expected 'to make its services self-supporting at the earliest possible moment'. And in the United States, in July 1925, a regular trans-continental air mail service was instituted by the US Post Office. Though the latter service encountered many vicissitudes, American enthusiasm for

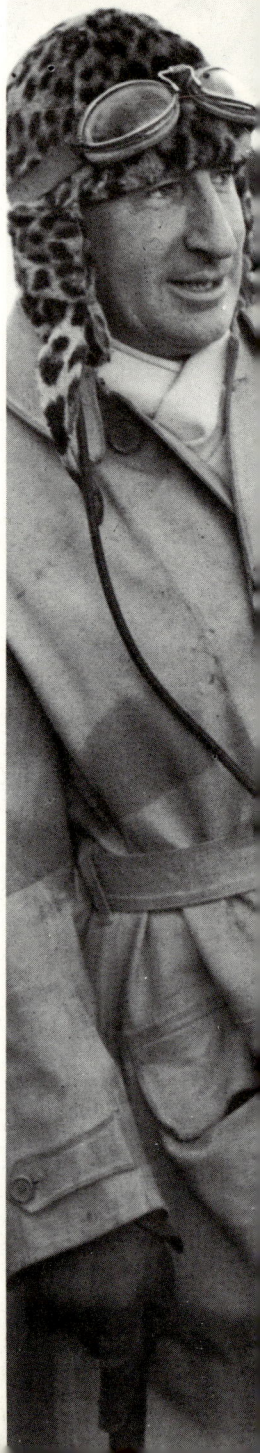

Right: Air Vice-Marshal Sir Sefton Brancker (wearing a monocle), the first Director-General of British Civil Aviation

commercial flight was not dimmed. In April 1925, for example, Henry Ford started a regular air freight service between Detroit and Chicago.

In the six years since the end of the war civil aviation had made enormous strides. There had been many long-distance pioneering flights, and a number of mail, freight, and passenger services were operating over shorter distances. The reliability of aero-engines had vastly improved and caused less anxiety during flights over long stretches of sea and desert or over dangerous mountain areas. Indeed, the regularity and safety of most of the air services was of a fairly high order.

But air travel and transport, though growing, had not as yet made any perceptible inroads on the older methods of sea and rail transport. The airways were still mainly for mails and for people in a hurry. Not even the most optimistic of air enthusiasts were then able to foresee the day when aircraft would largely supersede ships and trains over many of the world's routes.

Surveying the situation at the end of 1925 it is hard to believe that only a brief period of twenty-two years had elapsed since the historic flight by Wilbur and Orville Wright in their primitive biplane at Kitty Hawk. Perhaps at no other time in the history of mankind have such rapid and extensive advances been achieved by a single invention. In war the introduction of the third dimension by aircraft had revolutionised theory and eventually practice. In peace the changes were to be no less profound and far-reaching.

In the earlier days the prophets of air power and air transport were often thought to be overstating their case. They suffered scorn and ridicule. But even by 1925 very much of what they foresaw had been realised. Now, some forty-five years later, we can record that none of them, not even the boldest and most far-seeing, had been able to realise the full effect on human affairs of the conquest of the air and of the conquest of space that was to be its logical successor.

For mankind the development of aviation has not, perhaps, been an unmixed blessing, but it has conferred great advantages and opened up vast new fields of endeavour. Let us never forget that this great transformation has been mainly brought about by the courage, vision, and dedication of many thousands of enthusiasts the world over, a large number of whom lost their lives before they could see the fulfilment of their dreams.

Left: Speeding the post — an early England-India air mail plane

Chronology of events

1783 **19th September:** At Versailles the Montgolfier brothers—
Jacques and Joseph—send up a silk balloon filled with
hot air watched by Louis XVI and his court
21st November: Jean Pilâtre de Rozier and the Marquis
d'Arlandes ascend in a balloon above Paris, thus becoming the first men to fly through the air

1785 **7th January:** John Jefferies and Jean-Pierre Blanchard are
transported in a balloon across the English Channel from
Dover to Calais

1852 Henri Giffard constructs a man-carrying airship powered
by a 3 hp engine

1896 Otto Lilienthal, pioneer of gliding, killed during a
trial flight

1900 **2nd July:** First flight by a Zeppelin airship

1903 **17th December:** Orville and Wilbur Wright successfully
launch their motor-driven aircraft at Kitty Hawk, North
Carolina. Distance travelled: 852 feet.

1909 Louis Blériot flies across the English Channel

1912 **April:** The Royal Flying Corps is formed

1914 **July-August:** Outbreak of the First World War

1915 **19th January:** First Zeppelin raid on England
Anthony Fokker designs the interruptor gear which, by
giving the aeroplane efficient fire-power, finally makes
it an effective tactical weapon

1917 **April:** 'Bloody April' on the Western Front as the new
range of German aircraft practically sweep the Allied
air forces from the skies

1918 **1st April:** Formation of the Royal Air Force
21st April: The 'Red Baron', Manfred von Richthofen, is
killed in combat
November: End of the First World War

1919 **June:** John Alcock and Arthur Whitten-Brown fly non-stop
across the Atlantic from Newfoundland to Ireland
August: First commercial route between London and Paris
opened
November: Ross and Keith Smith fly from Britain to
Australia in a Vickers Vimy

1920 Croydon Airport designated London's terminus for Continental
air traffic

1921 In a series of aerial bombardment tests US general
'Billy' Mitchell sinks the ex-German warships *Frankfurt*
and *Ostfriesland,* and the USS *Alabama*

1925 Alan Cobham flies to Cape Town and back in a DH50

1926 **16th March:** American scientist Robert H.Goddard launches
the world's first liquid fuel rocket at Auburn, Mass.

*Top: Model of a parachute from a design by Leonardo da Vinci
(1452-1519) (left); 1919 advertisement from the famous Thomas
Cook travel agency (middle); walking, riding, and even flying
by steam—early 19th-century cartoon speculates on the
potential of the new steam power (right).* **Centre:** *Caricature of
the famous airship pioneer Alberto Santos-Dumont (left);
balloon display at Hurlingham, London, 1908 (middle); Maxim's
flying machine poised on its rail-runway, 1894 (right).* **Bottom:**
*American girl pilots, 1917 (left); hoisting a Sopwith from the
hold of a British aircraft carrier (middle); 1924 poster (right)*

The New Highway in the Air

AERIAL
TRAVEL
for
BUSINESS
or
PLEASURE

Preliminary Announcement by

THOS. COOK & SON
(F. H. COOK and E. E. COOK)
Chief Office : LUDGATE CIRCUS, LONDON, E.C.4

Index of main people, places, and events

Author's suggestions for further reading

A comprehensive history of the air war between 1914 and 1918 is contained in Walter Raleigh, *The War in the Air* (Oxford, 1922), vol. 1. J.P.Cuneo's *The Air Weapon, 1914-16* (Harrisburg, 1947), and R.P.Hearne's *Aerial Warfare* (London, 1919) are other useful contributions in the field. For a description of the greatest individual pilots of the war see Bruce Robertson, ed., *Air Aces of the 1914-1918 War* (Letchworth, 1959). In addition there are Hans Herlin's *Udet: A Man's Life* (London, 1960), and Edward V. Rickenbacker's personal account *Fighting the Flying Circus* (New York, 1919). Further interesting studies of the war period are M.Baring *RFC, HQ* (London, 1968), Heinz J.Nowarra, *Marine Aircraft of the 1914-1918 War* (Letchworth, 1966), D.H.Robinson, *The Zeppelin in Combat* (London, 1966), and Thomas H.Funderburk, *The Fighters* (New York, 1965).

Among the important figures of the post-war period, the work of Air Marshal Trenchard can best be studied in Andrew Boyle, *Trenchard* (New York, 1962). General 'Billy' Mitchell's career is reviewed in Isaac Don Levine, *Mitchell: Pioneer of Air Power* (Cleveland, 1944). A very useful work of general reference is L.G.S.Payne, *Air Dates* (London, 1957).

Library of the Twentieth Century will include the following titles:

Russia in Revolt
David Floyd
The Second Reich
Harold Kurtz
The Anarchists
Roderick Kedward
Suffragettes International
Trevor Lloyd
War by Time-Table
A.J.P. Taylor
Death of a Generation
Alistair Horne
Suicide of the Empires
Alan Clark
Twilight of the Habsburgs
Z.A.B. Zeman
Early Aviation
Sir Robert Saundby
Birth of the Movies
D.J. Wenden
America Comes of Age
A.E. Campbell
Lenin's Path to Power
G. Katkov and H. Shukman
The Weimar Republic
Sefton Delmer
Out of the Lion's Paw
Constantine Fitzgibbon
Japan: The Years of Triumph
Louis Allen
Communism Takes China
C.P. FitzGerald
Black and White in South Africa
G.H. Le May
Woodrow Wilson
E.A. Ions
France 1918-34
J.P.T. Bury
France 1934-40
W. Knapp
Mussolini's Italy
E.M. Robertson
The Little Dictators
A. Polonsky
Viva Zapata
L. Bethell
The World Depression
Malcolm Falkus
Stalin's Russia
A. Nove
The Brutal Reich
Donald Watt
The Spanish Civil War
Raymond Carr
Munich: Czech Tragedy
K.G. Robbins

Air Marshal Sir Robert Saundby, KCB, KBE, MC, DFC, AFC, DL served in the Royal Flying Corps as a fighter pilot during the First World War. After the war he continued in the RAF, among other assignments serving in Iraq, Aden, Egypt, and at the Air Ministry. In 1940 he was appointed Assistant Chief of the Air Staff, and promoted to Air Vice-Marshal. He was knighted in 1944, and promoted to Air Marshal. Invalided out of the service in 1946, he has maintained his close association with flying and with the RAF ever since.

JM Roberts, General Editor of the *Macdonald Library of the 20th Century,* is Fellow and Tutor in Modern History at Merton College, Oxford. He was General Editor of Purnell's *History of the 20th Century,* and is Joint-Editor of the *English Historical Review,* and author of *Europe 1880-1945* in the Longman's History of Europe. He has been English Editor of the *Larousse Encyclopedia of Modern History,* has reviewed for *The Observer, New Statesman,* and *Spectator,* and given talks on the BBC.

Library of the 20th Century

Publisher: John Thompson
Editor: Richard Johnson
Executive Editor: Peter Prince
Designed by: Brian Mayers/ Germano Facetti
Design: HCB Designs
Research: Mary Facetti

Pictures selected from the following sources:

Eugene Ankeny 122
Air France 115 116
BN EST 65
BOAC 65
Brown Brothers 29
Camera Press 77
Thos. Cook & Son 123
Crown Copyright 95 96 99
Deutsches Museum, Munich 31
Editions Rencontre 1
Etablissements cinematographi-
que des armées 59
Flight International 27 123
M.L.Guaita 7 47 66 70 72-3 122
Geo. Hun 122
Imperial War Museum 25 44 48 50
53 57 59 60 63 65 123
Keystone 92
Library of Congress 18
London Museum 12-13
Mansell Collection 8
Moro, Rome 54 80 83 86 90
National Archives, Washington 105
National Gallery of Canada,
Ottawa 69
Radio Times Hulton 14 23 65 86
108 115 119
Royal Aeronautical Society 10 14
21 123
Science Museum, London 11 35
123
Simplicissimus 37
Smithsonian Institution 16 24 25
57 108
Snark International 8
Sphere 84 110
Südd Verlag 38 55
Tate Gallery/John Webb 4
Ullstein 29 33 59 64 78
US Air Force 88 100-1
USIS 128
Vickers Ltd. 42
Zeppelin Museum, Ludwigshaven
25 31 50

*If we have unwittingly infringed copy-
right in any picture or photograph re-
produced in this publication, we tender
our sincere apologies and will be glad
of the opportunity, upon being satisfied
as to the owner's title, to pay an
appropriate fee as if we had been able
to obtain prior permission.*